Bt 4.13

D0884054

The Social Basis of American Communism

A VOLUME IN THE SERIES

COMMUNISM IN AMERICAN LIFE
Clinton Rossiter, General Editor

BOOKS PUBLISHED TO DATE:

The Roots of American Communism by Theodore Draper

The Communists and the Schools by Robert W. Iversen

The Decline of American Communism by David A. Shannon

American Communism and Soviet Russia by Theodore Draper

Marxism: The View from America by Clinton Rossiter

Communism and the Churches by Ralph Lord Roy

The Moulding of Communists by Frank S. Meyer

The Social Basis of American Communism by Nathan Glazer

Nathan Glazer

THE SOCIAL BASIS

OF AMERICAN

COMMUNISM

Harcourt, Brace & World, Inc. · *New York*

This book is one of a series of studies of Communist influence in American life. The entire survey has been made possible through the foresight and generous support of the Fund for the Republic. All of us who have taken part in it are grateful for this exceptional opportunity to study the most confused and controversial problem of the age and to publish the results exactly as we find them.

CLINTON ROSSITER

CONTENTS

TABLES

The Social Basis of American Communism

INTRODUCTION

C ommunism in America is a peculiar subject of study. From one point of view, it is difficult to see why it is of any great importance. The Communist Party achieved, even in its best days, only a tiny vote for its candidates. Its membership has never been large: even at its peak, there were considerably fewer than 100,000 Communists. Communism is, of course, given greater importance than its own achievements in America would warrant simply because American Communism is part of a great international power struggle. Thus, even a small Communist movement in America has a greater significance than more powerful domestic tendencies without such international links.

But there is a second reason why Communism—despite the relatively small number of Communists, the few votes cast for Communist candidates, and the almost universal opposition to Communism in the mass media—is important in America; and this is the peculiar nature of membership in the Communist Party. American Communism is worthy of the study that has been lavished on it because to be a Communist is not

3

the same thing as being a Democrat, a Republican, or a Socialist; a Catholic or a Jew; a trade-union member or a Chamber of Commerce member. To be a Communist means, ideally, and in large measure in reality, to be enlisted as a soldier in an organization. One hesitates to call it a "cause," because the cause has been changed so often in response to the needs of the Russian state. Yet it acts on those committed to it as powerfully as any cause, any movement, has in the past. Central to Communism is the organization; central to the organization are those committed to it, the formal members, who, when they accept the discipline and orders of their superiors, are called by the military term of "cadres."

The Communist Party, as the Communists were fond of saying (in America and elsewhere), was not like other parties. Its votes represented not even the smallest part of the iceberg of its influence, for it was only because of some general, centrally directed strategy that the Communists would even bother to put up candidates in any election. And certainly its membership was not like the membership of other parties and movements, for not only was it recruited in special ways, and in the light of central strategic considerations, but it was subject to special training, was treated by the leadership as a deployable resource, and was available for almost any objective. The difference between Communism and other parties, other movements, other faiths may perhaps be here exaggerated. But the more likely error is to underestimate this difference.

It is for these reasons that a special study of the membership of the Communist Party offers some advantages for the understanding of Communism in America. It is not an extravagant claim to assert that it is membership—or, rather better, tested and available and deployable membership—that is basically the chief aim of any Communist Party. At certain times and in certain places, the party aimed at the seizure of power. At all times and all places, it aimed at the advancement of Soviet interests. But for all its tasks, whatever they might be, the emphasis was on members—and this not as a symbol of success, or in a vainglorious desire to achieve large numbers, but because these members were the real strength and resources of the party. One cannot read Communist literature for any period of time without being impressed by the continual analysis of the problem of getting members, holding members, training members. Indeed, what others may see as the central objectives of the party—affecting public influence through a party or controlled press, capturing other organizations, forwarding certain policies—are, in the party literature, often viewed from this central perspective: Do they gain us new forces, do they train the existing forces, do they give us access to positions from which we may recruit new forces? [1]

The membership is the treasure of the party. It is consequently no academic exercise to examine this membership—to ask where it came from, how and why it was recruited, why members stayed and why others left. On the study of this "where" and "how" and "why" is it necessary to say a few more words.

Communism in America attracts or recruits only very small numbers. Since the experience of party recruitment, membership, and defection is so often intense and traumatic, the psychological aspects of this process have attracted a good deal of attention, and one major study of Communist Party membership is a psychological study.[2] It would seem reasonable if one studies human behavior and the behavior is rather eccentric, as measured by the behavior of most people, that attention should be directed to the individual psychology of the persons involved, and that something enlightening in their psychological processes would be found to explain the reasons for their behavior.

And yet, even though to be a Communist in America is on the whole exceptional and eccentric, considerable variation is found from one social group to another in the numbers that become Communists. The most important step to a proper understanding of the questions "who" became Communists and "why" is to realize that for certain social groups, for certain milieux, *it was neither eccentric nor exceptional to become a Communist.* The "normal" Communists, the Communists who joined the party in the course of a relatively common psychological development, far, far outnumber those who had exceptional and rare psychological reasons for joining.

It is certainly legitimate to ask, as many have asked, what are the psychological reasons people become Communists. Even if joining the party was a relatively common action, as it was in certain foreign-language groups, in certain unions, in certain professions at certain times and in certain places, there were still, among these groups, some who did join and some who did not. And there may well be matters of interest in the personal histories of members, their attitudes to family figures and authority, that will help explain their behavior. But a somewhat different approach may be to ask about Communists simply: "Who" are they, in terms of certain common social categories? And the answer to this question is also often an implied answer to the question: "Why" are they Communists?

This book thus takes what may be called a "sociological" approach, asking: Who were the Communists? I believe that in answering "who," I have also answered many questions about "why."

Each approach has its own virtues and defects. One virtue of the sociological approach is that its categories remain relatively unambiguous and unquestionably meaningful. The importance of class in explaining individual behavior does not have to be argued, even though it may be argued whether status or occupation or education is the best measure for determining a person's class, or whether it is a person's own class, his parents' class, or his expected final class that is the most relevant in explaining his behavior. Nor does it have to be argued, certainly not in America, that ethnic background and race are also important categories helping to explain individual behavior. Within these two large frames—the frame of class and the frame of ethnic background and race—most of what is said in this book can be encompassed. Obviously, when one tries to explain a person's behavior in terms of these gross divisions, one is, in effect, using a "psychology," but it is an unspecialized, a nontechnical psychology. It is the psychology that assumes that people act for their self-interest, as far as they can see it; and in this self-interest, motives of economic self-interest, of prestige, status, and self-respect, of emotional satisfaction are important.

The Communist Party was intensely interested in the "social composition" of its membership. Communist theory gave instructions as to where the Communist Party would and should find the greatest response to its appeals. The most exploited and the most oppressed had to be recruited, and it was the most exploited and the most oppressed who were also theoretically most ready to respond to Communist appeals. They, too, would make the best members, the best human material, the most dependable and the most loyal. The natural targets of the party were considered everywhere to be the industrial workers—and America was no exception to this general rule. In the United States, however, the immigrant make-up of the population and the presence of a large colored minority presented the party with both a complication and an opportunity. The complication was that the industrial working class was divided into many ethnic groups, and was largely made up of recent immigrants, only partially Americanized; the opportunity was provided by the Negroes.

Consequently, the two great targets of Communist efforts to recruit were the industrial workers, particularly the native and Americanized elements among them, and the Negroes. But American social reality, it turned out, showed that these groups did not fit into Communist theoretical categories. The greatest response did not necessarily come from the groups that were wooed most ardently. Therefore, groups that have not been assigned a major role in the Communist drama of history, but flocked into the party—professional and middle-class groups, and especially Jews among them—will be considered here, too.

In this book, I take up, roughly in chronological order, the groups from which the party got its greatest and most significant response. In the first chapter, I describe the elements—largely to be found in the Socialist Party of World War I—from which the first members of the Communist Party were drawn. In the second I discuss the immigrant workers who made up the greater part of the party during the twenties, and the problems their immigrant background created for the party. The third chapter is devoted to the party's efforts to recruit native-born workers and to penetrate and capture the trade unions; the fourth to the middle-class and professional groups that became increasingly prominent in the party in the late thirties and remained prominent through the forties. In the fifth I discuss the party's efforts to recruit Negroes, which began in the late twenties and early thirties, and became most intense after World War II and the opening of the cold war.

This book is not a complete survey of all the social groups to which Communists tried to appeal. At one time or another, they directed a special appeal and special efforts to almost every part of American society. Perhaps the most important omission here is the farmers. The party showed a continual interest in the poor farmers, and in the early years of the Depression was able to make contact with farmers and farm groups. However, its successes were so minor, its failure so complete, and the evidences of its role so fragmentary, that I decided to omit the farmers from this story of Communist Party membership.

Another social group not discussed at any length is that of intellectuals and cultural figures. In part, they are represented in the professional and middle-class groups discussed in Chapter IV. But no particular attention has been given to them. So much has been written on the special problem of the relation between intellectuals and the Communist Party that I have decided to limit myself to the larger social groups that contributed most significantly to party membership.[3]

The first chapter speaks of events that took place before the founding of the Communist Party in 1919, and the fourth and fifth chapters of events after the great decline in its membership in the early fifties. But most of the book deals with the period between 1920 and 1950. After 1950, under the pressure of government and trade-union attack, the party became rather small; after 1956-57, in consequence of Khrushchev's speech on Stalin's crimes and the Hungarian revolution, it became much smaller. While unquestionably it continued to recruit and gain members after 1950—and still does today—this recruitment is on such a small scale that it seemed reasonable to limit the main part of the story to the period when it was able to achieve a steady flow of new members.

I have often been asked, during the period when I worked on this book, "How do you get your information?" It has been surprising to me how many people, intelligent and well informed on other matters, believe that a study of the sort I have undertaken must be, if not impossible, very speculative. It is widely believed that the secrecy of the Communist Party, the sensation-seeking of Congressional investigations, and the unreliability of former Communists make a study of the membership of the Communist Party a risky and uncertain affair. As a matter of fact, the Communist Party has been remarkably unsecretive about the social characteristics of its membership; Congressional investigations have placed on the record a vast amount of reliable information; and many former Communists have been not only reliable witnesses on the American Communist Party, but important analysts of Communism. These are the three main sources for this study.

There exists, first of all, a large volume of publications by the Communist Party itself bearing on its membership. This literature consists of reports to conventions, reports to the Communist International and discussions in its periodicals, discussions in the important theoretical organ, *The Communist* (later *Political Affairs*), and in internal organizational publications—the *Party Organizer, Party Voice,* and others. How reliable is the information to be found in these publications? The discussions of membership, membership figures, and the responses of different social categories are designed specifically to guide the work of party members. They are meant to point out failings, and (less often) to commend successes. Of course, the names of specific individuals are not given—on this the party is secretive. Very often, the names of specific towns, specific factories and organizations are concealed. But there is little reason for such material to be imaginary or false. At times, there is some exaggeration, often enough revealed by internal evidence. On occasion, I have had access to documents meant for the eyes of top party leaders (Political Bureau minutes, an "Organization Conference" report of 1930, a report on membership and statistics for 1942). From these unpublished internal materials it may be discovered that the public materials of the same date on party membership correspond to the unpublished material; the figures have not been doctored, though only enough of them are published to support the arguments addressed to the members on the kind of activity that is most necessary. One cannot use party sources uncritically, and on occasion a pattern of concealment or direct falsification may be discovered. But I believe that the materials I have used are, on the whole, reliable.

There is by now an enormous literature resulting from Congressional investigations and government trials and hearings on the Communist Party and front organizations under the Smith Act and the McCarran-Walter Act. Again, the reliability of this material has been attacked, but generally, it appears to me, on insufficient grounds. Some witnesses have been unreliable, but little of this material has been successfully contradicted. The accounts, for example, of Communist influence in trade unions given by former Communists and anti-Communists parallel what was generally known by informed members of those unions and students of the labor movement, and have been supported by the material resulting from C.I.O. expulsions of Communist unions and in scholarly studies of these unions. No careful study of the Communist Party can afford to ignore these materials. My footnotes indicate the degree to which I have used them.

There is, finally, the vast secondary literature on the American Communist Party. Theodore Draper's two books, *The Roots of American Communism* and *American Communism and Soviet Russia* (New York: Viking, 1957 and 1960), form the definitive history of the party until the end of the 1920's; any writer on the Communist Party must lean heavily on this major work of historical scholarship. I have benefited, too, from these volumes of the Fund for the Republic's "Communism in American Life" series: Robert W. Iversen, *The Communists and the Schools,* David A. Shannon, *The Decline of American Communism,* Clinton Rossiter, *Marxism: The View from America,* and Ralph Lord Roy, *Communism and the Churches* (New York: Harcourt, Brace, 1959, 1959, 1960, and 1960). Also useful has been the general history by Irving Howe and Lewis Coser, *The American Communist Party* (Boston: Beacon, 1957) and the unpublished doctoral thesis of Francis X. Sutton, "The Radical Marxist" (Harvard University, 1950).

Aside from all written sources, there are the many people who have become experts on the American Communist Party or on some part of its history, some of whom were members of the Communist Party. I have spoken with many of these people, both informally and in formal interview, both generally and in search of information on specific points or to confirm written materials. Such interviews are referred to in the notes when they were the most important source for a point.

From the point of view of the sociologist, the perfect material for this study would be a statistically analyzed report based on a fully interviewed cross section of the Communist Party, made at intervals during the forty years of its existence. I believe this kind of data is literally impossible to get, though it might be approximated at great cost from information in the possession of the F.B.I. and the Communist Party. Yet I doubt that it would be worth the cost, for while it would improve the reliability of the picture of Communist Party membership given in this book, it would not change it radically. The sources described above are sufficient to get the essential parts of the story of the membership of the American Communist Party.

ONE · THE BACKGROUND OF COMMUNIST PARTY MEMBERSHIP

T he American Communist Party is a classic instance of the historical fact that most of the Communist parties that came into existence in the early twenties were formed out of Socialist parties. To understand the first members of the Communist Party, one must begin with the American Socialist Party. The composition of this party not only determined in large measure the initial social base of the Communist Party, but also set important lines for its potential growth; for it was former Socialists, in the twenties, who were the most likely targets for Communist organizational efforts, and the most likely recruits.

The Socialist Party of the United States at the outbreak of World War I had declined somewhat from the peak of its power. In 1912, it had 118,000 dues-paying members and polled for its candidate 6 per cent of the vote for President. By 1914, its membership had declined to 94,000,[1] but there was little feeling in the party that this was anything more than a temporary decline: the party was still intact, and still embraced a larger range of social elements than any other Marxist-influenced party has ever had in this country.

Particularly striking was the high proportion of native-born Americans who were members of the party and active in it. Indeed, in terms of the history of Marxist parties in the United States, the Socialist Party of 1901-18 appears as a surprising native interlude, sandwiched between two parties whose members were in overwhelming proportion immigrants. Preceding the Socialist Party was the Socialist Labor Party, which had hardly any English-speaking members (in 1891, only two members of its ruling committee spoke English); [2] succeeding it was a party that was overwhelmingly made up of the foreign-born.

Most of the leaders of the Socialist Party, from its founding convention in 1900 to the emergency convention of 1917, were native-born. [3] Outside the leadership group, there were much larger numbers of foreign-born; and among the working-class element of the party the foreign-born were very likely in the majority in 1914, and certainly in the majority by 1919. The native American members, on the other hand, were mostly of the middle class or farmers; few were industrial workers. I will attempt to characterize the size and quality of the different sections of the party. [4]

1) The Great Plains and Mountain states and the Far West supplied a remarkably large proportion of the membership and voting strength of the Socialist Party. Of the 94,000 members in 1914, Oklahoma had the surprising total of 7,000, Texas had almost 3,000, Kansas 2,000, Washington 3,200, California 5,300. Oklahoma was surpassed only by New York, with 10,700 members, and Pennsylvania, with 7,600. [5]

In 1912, the Socialists had gained in Oklahoma the highest percentage of any state's vote for their Presidential candidate.

Almost 17 per cent of the vote went to Eugene V. Debs. The party did almost as well in Nevada, and it also gained more than 10 per cent of the vote in Montana, Arizona, Washington, California, and Idaho.[6]

What explains this Socialist strength in Oklahoma and its Great Plains neighbors to the north and south, and the large Socialist vote in the Western states?

The strength in the Great Plains came largely from poor farmers. In Oklahoma, sentiment among the poor farmers was mobilized by a particularly skillful political organization, which borrowed techniques and personnel from the powerful Socialist organization of Milwaukee.[7] This Socialism was one of the series of radical political movements that the Great Plains farmers adopted with passion as a solution to their problems between the 1870's and the 1920's. Just before Socialism, had come Populism; just after it—in the northern Plains states— came the Non-Partisan League. In each case, these movements were seized upon as a means of achieving the special farmer's utopia of high prices and low costs.[8] Socialism placed less emphasis than Populism on monetary manipulation to achieve high prices, and more on political pressures to achieve low costs, but it fulfilled much the same function, for those who became Socialists, that Populism had before it.

These farmer Socialists had little of the interest and competence in socialist ideology that was so common among the Socialists of the Northeast and Midwest. Adopted in response to immediate economic needs, Great Plains Socialism had little staying power: as will be seen, an attachment to a minority political creed, like Socialism or Communism, that is based solely on economic causes—that is, on economic distress and the attempt to meet it—has no permanence in America. One needs a strong ideological basis of commitment to remain firm in the support of what are, in the American context, eccentric and exceptional creeds. Great Plains Socialism, which seemed so strong in 1914, was to wither almost completely within the next few years: there was hardly anything for the Communists to pick up there, either in 1919 or in later years. Yet, so volatile were the politics of the Great Plains farmers that even the Communist Party was able to get some response from them in the depths of the Depression of the thirties, though this limited Communist success of later years was in the northern Plains states, not in Oklahoma. The great Socialist organization of that state disappeared without a trace. Of the 11,000 Socialists in Oklahoma, Texas, and Kansas in 1914, there were hardly any ten years later, in either the Socialist or the Communist Party.

2) Quite different in character were the Socialists of the Mountain states and the Far West. These contributed the strongest native working-class element in the Socialist Party, and one that was to play an important role in the subsequent history of the American Communist Party. The workers of the Western states were largely Anglo-Saxon and Irish in origin. They had first been drawn by the gold rush to California and then by other mining strikes to other Western states, and only gradually and reluctantly accepted the necessity of working for wages. These workers did not conceive of themselves at first as wageworkers; many were disappointed fortune seekers, with a good deal of self-reliance, and with special knowledge of the use of weapons and dynamite. As Vernon H. Jensen wrote:

> Only a few among the multitudes who rushed out after fortune found it. The majority became workers, especially if they stayed. These men made up a distinctive labor force different from that which was gradually introduced through the later influx of immigrants . . . independent men who set out early to strike it rich had profound influence on employer-worker relations for many years.[9]

The lumbermen, seamen, longshoremen, and agricultural workers thus contained large numbers of native Americans, of English-speaking immigrants, of fortune seekers, of independent-minded men acquainted with violence. In all these occupations, and in mining as well, large numbers of immigrants soon made their appearance. Perhaps nothing so makes for radicalism as the disappointment of hopes for great success within a system of free enterprise. The homesteading farmers who had hoped to strike it rich on the plains were ready to turn to almost any wild political venture in their frustration; the same seemed true for the Western miners. However, there were a number of differences which made this Western working-class group a much more persistent radical element, whether in the Socialist Party, the Industrial Workers of the World, or the Communist Party, than the farmers.

Most important, perhaps, in establishing the radicalism of Western miners was the existence, from the early 1890's on, of the Western Federation of Miners, one of the strongest prewar American unions, and one of the most radical. Here the sentiments bred by frustration and exploitation were harnessed within an organizational form. In 1905, the Western Federation of Miners helped organize the Industrial Workers of the World, which, to the radical miners, added lumber workers, agricultural workers, and others. This was another organizational frame supporting Western Socialism.

But in addition to organization, there was also ideology. The Western Federation of Miners was remarkable in that almost from the beginning of its organization it was concerned with creating an all-embracing labor organization along industrial lines which would have larger and more radical goals than the unions of the American Federation of Labor. It was because of this interest that it helped form the I.W.W.

The W.F.M. steadily attempted to expand into more than just another labor union, to develop a new form of unionism which might have enormous power in society. Part of the explanation of its radicalism is undoubtedly to be found in the social circumstances of miners. They generally live in communities in which they form the entire working-class group, they work in large groups, and they generally confront a single employer.[10] All these circumstances would tend to increase class consciousness. But it should also be noted that this remarkably mixed working class, drawn from varied elements throughout the country and throughout the world, harbored individuals who had had some contact with the brands of radical and working-class ideology then current.[11] These fragments of ideology helped bring the leaders of the W.F.M. into national radical politics, and into contact with such sophisticated Easterners as Daniel De Leon, head of the Socialist Labor Party. The sophisticated Eastern radicals soon taught the Westerners everything they did not know about socialism, syndicalism, anarchism, and the rest.

Economic need alone is an inadequate spur to permanent attachment to a radical party in America. But the combination of organization and ideology is the solidest base for such attachment. This existed in the Mountain states and the Far West, though the Communists were at first able to do little about the potential there. While the Socialism of the Plains states was to leave nothing for the Communist Party to inherit or capture, the socialism of Western workingmen was to present a fertile field and, in time, to supply one of the largest parts and strongest sections of the native base of the Communist Party.

Saying "Western," however, does not automatically mean "native." It is true that the working class in the Western states numbered a smaller proportion of immigrants and foreign-born than in the East, and yet the West, too, was attractive to immigrants. The difference was that in the West they could not often form large, homogeneous colonies, using their own language, reading their own newspapers, and remaining relatively impervious to ideological and institutional influences coming from the outside. There, the immigrant was more completely removed from his European past, and his orientation was not that of a member of a special ethnic group. In a word, he was more assimilated, and even though he may have formed a sizable proportion of the workers in certain areas, the stamp of the working-class group in the West generally remained native American.

3) A third important native element in the Socialist Party was the middle class. Socialists were dotted here and there through the middle classes of almost every American small town. In addition, reformers of all types had flocked into the party. It was often not easy to draw lines between the different kinds of reform current in the hectic period from the turn of the century to World War I, between atheists and agnostics, evolutionists and ethical culturists, utopians and currency reformers, fighters for women's rights and for children's rights. While the majority of these were not Socialists, many of them added Socialism to the list of worthy causes, subscribed to a newspaper or magazine, voted for the party, and perhaps became members. The early pages of Mother Bloor's autobiography give an engaging picture of this swirl of reform, and show how often one went from one movement to another, and then on to Socialism, or combined three or four, including Socialism.[12]

The Socialist Party also included large numbers of teachers, lawyers, and even clergymen—there were 300 clergymen members of the party in 1908.[13] There were numerous Socialist journalists and writers and lecturers, many of whom indeed

could make a living working on Socialist newspapers and maga-
zines, writing for the Socialist press, lecturing before Socialist
audiences. In 1912, five Socialist dailies in English and eight
foreign-language dailies were being published, as well as 262
English weeklies and 36 foreign weeklies, ten English monthlies
and two foreign monthlies.[14] (Mother Bloor at one point supported herself and her children by writing for Socialist maga-
zines.[15]) A Socialist convention reflected the prominence of
middle-class people and intellectuals in the party. Of 294 delegates in 1912, no less than 32 were newspapermen, and 21
lecturers; 20 were lawyers, and 60 were in such categories as
manufacturers, real-estate brokers, retail merchants, authors,
ministers, physicians and dentists.[16]

4) The "shock troops" of the Socialist Party—that is, the
elements that stuck with it the longest, that showed the smallest
number of defections, that supplied much of the money and a
good deal of the manpower—were the Jewish workers of New
York and other Northeastern and Midwestern cities, and the
German workers of Milwaukee and other Midwestern and Eastern cities. Other ethnic groups also supplied important contingents to the Socialist Party—in particular, the Finns—but they
fall into a somewhat different category from the group now
under discussion and will be taken up later.

Socialism was an international movement, stronger almost
everywhere in Europe than in America. Naturally, it had a considerable influence on immigrants to America. During the period
before World War I, the heaviest immigration in American history took place, sometimes reaching a million a year. Generally,
the earlier immigrants in each ethnic group came from the land,
and were more influenced by tradition and religion, while later,
because Europe was industrializing and urbanizing as fast as
America, they came in larger and larger proportions from the

cities. Consequently, while a German immigrant of the 1850's was likely to be a peasant or village artisan, one of the 1890's was more likely to be an industrial worker from a city. The only major exception to this pattern was the Jews, who did not supply any peasant element at all.

Many of the immigrant workers who entered the Socialist Party in America had been Socialists in Europe, though many others discovered Socialism for the first time in America. The conditions of immigrant workers were worse than those of native-born workers; they had poorer jobs, received lower wages, found it much more difficult to become foremen and skilled workers. However, the circumstances of their lives had less to do with *making* them Socialists than with *keeping* them Socialists. Indeed, Socialism very likely lost more adherents among the immigrants than it gained.[17] In this country, many shopkeepers, property owners, and manufacturers who had been Socialists in their youth abandoned their old faith. The biography of almost every immigrant labor leader or radical shows that the first contact with radicalism came in Europe.[18] It is very likely that more American Socialists were made in Warsaw and Lodz than in New York.

In sum, the major part of the immigrant working-class base of the American Socialist Party had been workers in Europe, and had first come into contact with radical working-class movements there. In fact, their leaders were often forced to emigrate because of their activities in organizing unions and radical parties.

In America, this group formed excellent material for the building of trade unions and Socialist parties. They were accustomed to expressing their outlook through organization. The Jewish needle-trade workers of New York were solidly organized by World War I in the International Ladies' Garment

Workers' Union, the Amalgamated Clothing Workers Union, and in the furriers' and hatters' unions. All these organizations were avowedly Socialist: their members read Socialist newspapers, many of them studied Socialist doctrine, their leaders were important members of the Socialist Party. German workers were organized in locals of various craft unions (printers, bakers, brewers, and others) and were almost as commonly Socialist in outlook: older immigrants and skilled workers, their Socialism was more moderate. They formed that iron combination of ideology and organization which is extremely difficult to break up and which makes the securest base for radical political activity.

In the Socialist Party of 1914, the membership in the Northeastern and Midwestern states was largely of this type. It included Jews, Germans, Poles, Czechs and Slovaks, Hungarians, South Slavs, and many others, but the Jewish and German contingents were at this time the most important.

5) The immigrant workers just discussed were those who soon spoke English and who participated in the regular work of the party. Later immigrant groups, however, formed parties or groupings that were still related to the Socialist parties of their respective countries, of which so many had been members. These federations of immigrant workers played a special role in American Socialism. Many of them wanted to forge some fraternal link with the American Socialist Party, and out of this desire a new organizational form developed.

The pathbreakers were the Finnish Socialists. They were a relatively recent immigrant group: the peak of Finnish immigration was in the years 1899-1904.[19] The leading authority on American Finnish Socialism writes: "Immigrant socialism was for many years a child of the old country. . . . As the new gospel's first apostle testified, 'Socialism is with us a kind of immigrant baggage.' " [20] As with other ethnic groups, Socialism was part of a whole complex break with old traditions. The first Finnish Socialists preached atheism and science as well as Socialism, and their membership strength derived from anti-clericalism as well as from any specific grievances as working-men.

Many immigrants were in the throes of unsettling intellectual fer-ment, ready to grasp any unfamiliar or bizarre idea coming their way; they had long chafed under the stern ethic of conservative churches and temperance societies, and were eager to find a more liberal code . . . grocers, clothing merchants, land-agents, steam-bath proprietors, boardinghouse keepers, newspapermen—indeed a wide assortment of elements shortly to be denounced as petit-bourgeois—took ritualistic membership oaths in the Socialist party and found themselves seated next to honest-to-goodness laborers at meetings of the workingmen's clubs.[21]

Socialism in other ethnic groups, too—in particular, the Jewish—very often had this national character and tended to embrace large parts of a community, not only its workers. The "petit-bourgeois" elements were as convinced Socialists as the workers. And even when not, the life of the party or club was so important that it took more than disagreement with ideology to cause a storekeeper or small manufacturer who was a Social-ist to leave the group.

In 1904, the Finnish Socialists made overtures to the Socialist Party for a procedure whereby they might affiliate. The problem was how to avoid the payment of double dues, for the Finnish Socialists already supported their own local groups and national body, and it seemed unreasonable for them to have to pay full dues to the American Socialist Party, too. A means of affiliation was worked out in 1906, under which the Finnish Federation established a translator in the national office of the Socialist

Party to translate all the official acts of the party and make them known to the members of the federation, and a small sum was paid to the party by the federation for each of its members. In 1910, a regular means of affiliation for foreign-language federations was established, based roughly on this approach, with the national office paying the translator, presumably out of the per capita dues it received from the federations.[22]

The Finnish and Lettish groups were affiliated with the party by 1910. In the next year, South Slavic, Italian, and Scandinavian groups affiliated; in 1912, Hungarians and Bohemians came in; in 1913, Germans, Poles, Jews, and Slovaks; and in 1915, Ukrainians, Lithuanians, and Russians.[23] The Finnish group was by far the largest: in 1913, it had reached a membership of 14,000—though large sections later split away as a result of a schism over the I.W.W., and in 1917 it had only 9,400 members. The next largest groups in 1913 were the German, with over 5,000 members, and the Jewish, with 3,200.[24] But there were far more German and Jewish members in the party than in their respective federations. It was the less-assimilated, more newly arrived immigrants who participated in the party by way of the foreign-language federations. Many immigrants who had arrived young, the children of immigrants, and the more-assimilated immigrants were not members of foreign-language federations. A Morris Hillquit or an Ab Cahan, a Victor Berger or an Oscar Ameringer, though born in Eastern and Central Europe, did not operate in the Socialist Party as members of foreign-language federations.

In 1917, 33,000 of 80,000 party members were affiliated by way of foreign-language federations.[25] Despite the relatively large proportion of the total membership of the Socialist Party organized in foreign-language federations, these federations played little role in the party itself. The members were willing second-class members, and generally more concerned with their own organizations and their varied social activities—clubs, news-papers, schools, and the like—than with the general policies of the Socialist Party. Thus, even though the Finnish Federation numbered 10 per cent of the party from 1912 on, no leader of the Socialist Party of any importance came from the Finnish Federation. The foreign-language federations were to play a decisive role in the organization of the two Communist parties that were formed in 1919 out of the Socialist Party, but as late as 1917-18 they played no important role in the Socialist Party itself. The emergency convention of 1917 consisted over-whelmingly of native-born delegates, and represented native-born and somewhat-more-assimilated foreign-born members.

How can the significance of this large proportion of foreign-born in the membership of the Socialist Party be judged? Taking the point of view of an American party, competing in the politi-cal arena for votes, the Socialist leaders were happy to be so solidly based on native-born elements, and looked with some concern at the rising proportion of the foreign-language federa-tions. From the point of view of a Marxist party attempting to embrace the largest numbers of industrial workers, there was nothing exceptional in this strong foreign-born element. Indeed, it might be argued that if the American Socialist Party had been more truly representative of the industrial proletariat of America in the first decade and a half of the twentieth century, it would have been in even larger measure an organization of the foreign-born. The historian Ira Kipnis, who criticizes the party from the "Left," includes in his indictment its failure to bring in more foreign-born workers.[26] One central fact about the American working class in this period, and during subsequent decades, too, must be remembered: it was largely composed of immigrants. The working force in the steel mills, the coal mines, the textile factories, the clothing shops was overwhelmingly foreign-born, and that part of it that was not was concentrated in supervisory jobs and in the more highly paid skilled occupations:

The immigrant factor in the industrial labor supply became so important between 1900 and 1914 that in many industries the manual occupations were almost entirely filled by immigrants. The report of the United States Immigration Commission (1911) records . . . that only one-fifth of the total number of wage-earners in 21 principal branches of industry were native whites (of native-born parents). Almost three-fifths were of foreign birth; 17 per cent were the children of immigrants, and the other 5 per cent were Negroes.[27]

All these elements could be found in the Socialist Party on the eve of World War I, but they were not, of course, stable in their sizes and proportions and reflected changing social trends within the United States itself. In general, the Western and Plains parts of the party, the native-born and old immigrant sections, were on the verge of decline; while the new immigrant groups, and, in consequence, the Northeastern part of the party, was, relatively, increasing in strength.

Two other radical organizations existed alongside the American Socialist Party in the early 1900's. And when Communism came to power in Russia and looked for foreign allies, they both seemed promising sources of members for a new revolutionary party. One of these was the Socialist Labor Party, which, from the perspective of Moscow, seemed a sound revolutionary organization. From the perspective of New York, it clearly offered nothing. Daniel De Leon's party had by 1917 become the fossilized dogmatic sect it has remained to this day. It had 3,000 members,[28] and it is doubtful whether, surrounded by the iron shell of their peculiar ideology, more than a few of them ever emerged to join the Communist Party.

The other possible quarry for a new revolutionary party was much more promising: the Industrial Workers of the World. This organization had had a remarkably stormy history, even for the radical Left in America. From its foundation in 1905 until 1912, it had maintained a close but ambiguous relationship to the Socialist Party. Most of its leaders rejected political activity, emphasized sabotage and violence, and dismissed any thought of working within the regular established unions. All this was in opposition to the attitude of the majority of the Socialist Party. The party generally took the stand that trade-union affairs were none of the party's business—all it wanted from the trade unions was that they should politically support the party's effort to achieve socialism. Most of the trade-union people in the Socialist Party were connected with unions in the American Federation of Labor, and naturally opposed the I.W.W. for "dual unionism," because the I.W.W. operated in complete disregard of the jurisdictional rights and claims of established unions.

Despite this division between the Socialist Party and the I.W.W., in the early years the I.W.W. leaders were members of the party, and found it possible to remain within the one big family of the American Left. But in 1912, after the I.W.W. had had its greatest success, in leading the strike of the Lawrence, Massachusetts, textile workers, the I.W.W. and the Socialist Party came to the parting of the ways. William D. ("Big Bill") Haywood, leader of the I.W.W., and a member of the National Executive Committee of the Socialist Party, was attacked for his purported advocacy of violence (instead of political activity), and, by a vote of the membership, was recalled from the committee. The vote of the membership—23,500 to 11,000—

showed that Haywood's greatest strength was in the West, with Montana, Nevada, Oregon, Utah, Washington, and Texas voting for him. West Virginia and Tennessee also went for Haywood; and it might be argued that the mining–mountain–native-born complex makes these states somewhat "Western." The heaviest votes against him came in New York, Massachusetts, Pennsylvania, and Wisconsin.[29]

As a result of Haywood's recall, a good number of members of the I.W.W. withdrew from the party. However, many of them had never been members; and some who were members undoubtedly maintained their association with the party: there was no drastic decline in the membership rolls in the Western states. One of the heaviest membership losses clearly attributable to the fight with the I.W.W. was that of 3,500 Finns, centered in the Lake Superior region.[30]

But what did the I.W.W. membership consist of, and what did it offer a new revolutionary party? Estimates of I.W.W. membership fluctuated as wildly as did the membership itself, for the organization was capable of enrolling thousands of members during a successful strike and of losing them all within a short time after it was over. For the same year, 1913, one finds estimates ranging from 15,000 to 60,000 members. Perhaps it is reasonable to estimate some 15,000 activists in the first years of the World War, but to add that 300,000 membership cards had been issued between its founding in 1905 and the beginning of 1917, and this represented many tens of thousands of American and immigrant workers who had in some way been touched by this organization.[31]

The I.W.W. was certainly a more "American" organization, in terms of ideology and organization, than the Marxist-influenced parties. Its tactics arose out of the struggles of Western miners and migratory workers against their employers, and it owed almost nothing to European ideas. However, its membership was, if anything, more heavily foreign-born than that of the Socialist Party. Insofar as it organized workers in the East, it organized foreign-born workers; and even in the West, it dealt with relatively large numbers of the foreign-born—Finnish and Scandinavian miners and lumber workers in the Northwest, Mexican agricultural workers in California, and others. In 1917, it published newspapers in Russian, Bulgarian, Polish, Lithuanian, Finnish, Swedish, and Yiddish.[32] Its native American ideological orientation seemed to hinder it not at all in its approach to immigrant workers:

In its effort to reach immigrants through both written and oral propaganda the I.W.W. particularly excelled. . . . Propaganda nuclei were organized among practically every immigrant nationality. Literature was printed in various languages—Finnish, Italian, Russian, Hungarian, Bulgarian, Polish, Lithuanian, Croatian, Bohemian, and even Chinese. . . . With its foreign language pamphlets, books, press, and magnetic speakers, who invariably approached the immigrant workers sympathetically, it made tremendous inroads among them.[33]

Class and ethnic character (including race) are the two great systems of social division in American life, and in considering the impact of any political movement on American society, both systems must be kept in mind. Ethnic background was a more marked basis for division in 1914 than it is today, for that was the year the greatest migration of Europeans to this country in our history was brought to a temporary stop. But class, too, was a more marked basis for division at that time. And the two were more closely related than they are today, with ethnic stratification closely paralleling class stratification.

•

Two American Communist parties were formed in 1919 in response to the Bolshevik revolution of November 1917 and the establishment by the Russian Communists of a Third International in early 1919. The Communist International called on Socialists throughout the world to turn on their "Right-Wing" and "Centrist" leaders, organize parties on the Bolshevik pattern, and enter the Communist International. In the United States, its summons was addressed to four groups: the Left Wing of the American Socialist Party, the Industrial Workers of the World, the Socialist Labor Party, and the Workers International Industrial Union, a splinter from the I.W.W.[34] Of these groups, it was the Left Wing of American Socialism that responded to create American Communism.

Many individual issues had served in the years preceding World War I to define a Left Wing in the American Socialist Party.[35] They stemmed primarily from the division existing in Socialism between a revolutionary and apocalyptic perspective and a reformist and gradualist perspective. Out of these two large orientations came divisions between those who emphasized violence and those who emphasized vote-getting (as in the struggle over the recall of Bill Haywood); between those who wished to set up independent revolutionary unions and those who saw the Socialists as good citizens of existing unions; between those who emphasized the role of workers battling employers and those who emphasized the role of careful political organization.

It is not possible to draw strict parallels between the Left in the American Socialist Party and the Left in other prewar Socialist parties. The conflict in the German party between Karl Kautsky's Marxist orthodoxy and Eduard Bernstein's revisionism meant little here. Even though Victor Berger called himself "the American Bernstein," he tended here to be the ally of "the American Kautsky," Morris Hillquit, in the joint fight against the wild men from the West. Nor could meaningful echoes of the division between Mensheviks and Bolsheviks be found; here, the Left generally took, if anything, a Menshevik (liberal) attitude on organization, while the Right took a more Bolshevik attitude. The tone of the American Left was quite different from the tone of the Left in other Socialist parties. Its dominant note was the emphasis on a somewhat undisciplined violence, arising from the experience of native and immigrant workers in Western mining and lumber camps and Eastern mines and textile mills. This specific historical setting gave a strong assist to syndicalist and anarchist ideas, but these had nothing to do with either the German or the Russian Left. The similarity to the French Left, which was little known and had little influence in America, seems accidental.

Whether independently of the war these issues would have led to a break in the Socialist Party and the creation of a more radical group to its left is impossible to say. However, such a group, if it had been formed on the basis of the issues of 1912-14, would have been very different indeed from the Communist movement that was actually created in 1919. More important for the birth of American Communism than the fight over a political versus a direct-action approach was World War I.

In Europe, the war shattered the Socialist parties. Antiwar sentiment had been an important part of the Socialist appeal. The Socialist International had declared that its individual parties would not support their countries if they went to war. Yet, at the outbreak of war, the Socialist parties supported their national governments. In each party small minorities of anti-war Socialists fought the "defensist" and "patriotic" majorities.

In the beginning, it seemed that these splits would not affect the American Socialist Party. It was fortunate in being located in a country that was, first of all, not in the war, and in which, consequently, any position could safely be adopted. This was also a country that could not be threatened by invasions, and in which, therefore, no conflict between patriotism and Socialism arose. The American Socialist Party could thus maintain the antiwar position of the Second International with less inner struggle than could the Socialist parties of Europe.

Though it was easy for American Socialists to be doctrinairely antiwar, it was impossible to control, and perhaps even envisage, the remarkable consequences for the social composition of the Socialist Party that resulted from such a stand. The antiwar position of the party inevitably affected its different segments in different ways. In both World Wars, it became clear that a decisive factor determining one's position on American participation was ethnic background. Those of German origin in the party had good reason, aside from Socialism, to be antiwar; and there was no reason for them to defect from an antiwar party. The war affected the East European elements more variably. The Socialist immigrants coming from Czarist Russia looked forward to the overthrow of the Czar. One defeat in 1905 had almost brought down the repressive empire; what might not another defeat do? Jews, Poles, Lithuanians, Estonians, Latvians, Ukrainians, Finns, and even Russians looked forward to the collapse of the Czarist empire; [36] obviously, they could see no point to America entering the war on its side, particularly when all their ideological preconceptions were in opposition to entry into war in any case.[37] There was no reason for immigrants from Russia to leave the Socialist Party because of its antiwar stand: on the contrary, many joined on just this basis.

Nor was there much change in the antiwar position of these elements as a result of the February revolution in Russia and America's entry into the war. Many of the immigrants from

Russia were as much anti-Russian as anti-Czarist, and could see little point to a rapid turnabout from revolutionary defeatism to "defensism" because a bourgeois liberal regime of Great Russians had now replaced the Czar. To many doctrinaire Socialists, the governments of Prince Lvov and Alexander Kerensky were not sufficiently different from the Czar's to demand an about-face.[38] In any case, the fall of the Czar did not affect the position of the Socialist Party in the slightest, nor did America's entry into the war. In the fall of 1917, Morris Hillquit, running for mayor of New York City, got one of the biggest Socialist votes in any New York election on an antiwar platform—or, rather, on a platform as antiwar as seemed safe in view of the fact that he could easily have been indicted for sedition.[39] He received four times as many votes as the previous Socialist candidate for this office.[40]

Meanwhile, the war had quite a different impact on other elements in the party. In particular, some of the leading publicists and intellectuals in the party felt strongly that the United States was correct to enter the war on the side of England and France, and many leading figures of the middle-class intelligentsia left the party.[41] The predominantly Anglo-Saxon background of this element of the party cannot be ignored. In general, the party was weakened in the West and in the Great Plains states and became stronger in the East.[42] While there was strong antiwar sentiment among the native element of the party, the disappearance of Socialist influence in Oklahoma and elsewhere on the Plains within a few years of the end of the war suggests that, in addition to the rise in agricultural prices, the hardly conscious attachment of Americans of Anglo-Saxon origin to England must have played some role.

The rapid changes that took place in the composition of the American Socialist Party between 1917 and 1919 are most important for any understanding of the initial resources of the Communist Party. In a word, the middle-class, native-born base of the Socialist Party disintegrated. By 1917, the party had declined to 80,000 members, though in November 1917, it scored striking electoral successes in New York, Chicago, and other cities with large groups of foreign-born. The party's membership was beginning to rise in 1918 (after reaching a trough of only 75,000 members). This rise was based not on the old catchall reforming Socialist appeal, but on the basis of its antiwar position, and it was a rise that was largely concentrated in the East European–language federations. In 1917, the foreign-language federations, despite the fact that they held 33,000 of 80,000 members, played almost no role in the party. The Russian Federation was so unimportant that the *American Labor Year Book, 1917-1918* does not give any membership figure for it. The average monthly membership figure of the Russian Federation for the year ending March 1918 was only 792;[43] by December 1918, it had 2,400 members; by April 1919, 7,800 members.[44] In those few months, the membership of the Ukrainian Federation rose from 2,400 to 3,800, that of the South Slavic from 1,200 to 3,100, that of the Lithuanian from 4,800 to 6,000. These four federations alone increased their membership from 10,800 to 20,700 members. By April 1919, the party had increased to 108,500 members; 57,000, or 53 per cent, were in foreign-language federations.[45]

The reasons for this remarkable rise in the foreign-language federations are not completely clear. In most of these ethnic groups, religious and conservative elements were quite important, more important in terms of numbers and influence than the Socialists and other radicals. These elements could only have reacted in horror to Bolshevism, even (and particularly) early Bolshevism. The conservative and religious parts of the ethnic communities stemming from the border areas of the Russian empire only added to their antipathy for the Great Russians a hatred for the new revolutionary gospel.

However, the Socialist elements of these communities reacted with hysterical enthusiasm. The first great revolution promised by Socialist ideology had occurred in Russia, and it took a few years before it was completely clear to Socialists how different it was in many respects from the revolution they had envisaged. The last had become the first. The country that had oppressed Socialists most severely had now become the center from which Socialism and revolution would spread. The Bolsheviks, with their uncompromising opposition to war for any national purpose, were in the best position to capture those who were violently antiwar, and who saw the parties of the Second International as the betrayers of Socialism and the supporters of national defense. And it was the Socialists from the minority groups of the Russian empire who were most violently antiwar.

The Socialist Party of America, as has been said, was antiwar—among the most antiwar Socialist parties in the world. It never wavered from this position, even when its leaders were arrested for opposition to war. So, for the antiwar, pro-Bolshevik Socialists from Eastern Europe, the Socialist Party was a perfect home. They flocked into it, as nonimmigrant, prowar elements streamed out.

All this, however, does not completely explain the rapid rise in membership of the East European federations in the Socialist parties. The most rapid rise in membership, as previously indicated, was concentrated in the months after December 1918, a year after the Bolshevik revolution, and after the end of the war. The end of the war changed little, in terms of the significance of antiwar feeling, for the Socialist Left: arrest and trial for opposing the war still continued. And the end of the war in no way changed the position of the embattled Bolsheviks, who still had a variety of opposing armies to contend with.

However, in the light of these peculiarities of chronology it does not seem possible to explain the rapid rise of membership in the East European Socialist federations simply in terms of antiwar and pro-Bolshevik feeling. The issues played an important role; but more than issues was involved. For example, the Lettish Federation was the most antiwar, the most pro-Bolshevik of all, with close associations with the Russian Bolsheviks, and is the group to which Theodore Draper traces the first organizational seed of the Communist Party in America.[46] Yet the Lettish Federation increased its membership hardly at all in the four months that saw such rapid leaps for the Russians, Ukrainians, South Slavs, and Lithuanians. The membership of the Lettish Federation rose only from 1,353 to 1,606 between December 1918 and April 1919.[47] Were Letts less responsive to the Bolshevik revolution than other border peoples of the Russian empire? Hardly.

What this should suggest, it would seem, is that no analysis of relatively small social movements—and the history of the Communist Party in America is one of very small social movements—can be complete in terms of the social characteristics of groups, and their response to given issues. The significance of organizational factors in distinguishing the Socialism of different social groups in the Socialist Party has been referred to. Similarly, each of these ethnic groups had its own special organizational history—unfortunately, for the most part unwritten. The rapid increase in the membership of certain federations in the Socialist Party must also be understood in terms of organizational factors, which is often only a way of saying personal factors. The presence of an energetic group of leaders with organizational skills, capable of capitalizing on an issue and using it to increase their organization's strength, is a factor that inevitably differentiates group from group. Very likely these differences in organizational skill and capacity themselves reflect certain social characteristics of the group. But from the point of view of an analysis in terms of issues, and how they make an impact on one group or another, the differences in organizational potential between one group and another are accidental.

It is for this reason that it would be fruitless to attempt to explain in any detail, using issues and general social character alone, such a phenomenon as the rapid rise of membership in certain Socialist federations in the period just before the breakup of the party. Issues and social character set broad lines within which differences in organizational character, themselves often dependent on accidents of personality, produced different effects.

In late 1919, a group of East European foreign-language federations of the Socialist Party, together with some native American intellectuals and radicals, founded American Communism. Initially, two parties were formed, but after a few turbulent years, a single American party, part of the world-wide Communist Party centered in Moscow, was created.

TWO · FOREIGN-BORN WORKERS AND THE PARTY IN THE TWENTIES

$\mathbf{T}$he most striking characteristic of Communist Party membership throughout the twenties was that it was overwhelmingly composed of relatively recent immigrants. Probably only one in ten of the members was a native American. The immigrant members form the subject and the problem of this chapter.

I do not plan to retell here a story which has been recounted many times, and well: of the creation of two Communist parties —the Communist Labor Party and the Communist Party—in September 1919; of the government raids that drove them underground almost immediately; of their partial merger under Comintern pressure in the United Communist Party in 1920 and their more complete merger into a Communist Party of America in 1921; of the formation of a public and legal duplicate of this latter group—the Workers Party—at the end of 1921; and of the establishment of the Workers Party as the only American Communist Party with the dissolution of the underground Communist Party of America in April 1923.

The changes in the membership of these groups were less kaleidoscopic than their organizational history: it was very much the same group of members that took out cards in the successive parties, and that formed the base of the party throughout the twenties. There were changes, of course; in particular, in the earliest years many Russian Communists returned to Soviet Russia and depleted this section of the membership.[1] But much the same pool of members was drawn upon with each organizational change.

The great majority of these members came from the Socialist Party. In January 1919, this party had almost 110,000 members. In May and June of that year, great blocs of the membership were expelled or suspended for allegiance to the Left Wing that was forming in response to the Bolshevik revolution. By July 1919, the membership of the party was down to 40,000.[2] The two Communist parties were formed in September 1919 in Chicago primarily from this reservoir of 70,000 expelled or suspended members. One, the Communist Party, was based almost entirely on the expelled foreign-language federations; the other, the Communist Labor Party, had a somewhat greater proportion of native-born or English-speaking members. The Communist groups were driven underground at the beginning of 1920, and they stayed underground through 1920 and 1921, only sending up the "periscope" of the Workers Party at the end of 1921. As the entire party emerged from underground, it had about 12,000 members. At this time, in 1922, the Socialist Party had about the same number of members.[3]

In 1923, the Workers Party reported an average membership of 15,400; in 1924, 17,400; in 1925 (first half of the year), 16,300.[4] At this point, owing to a reorganization which will be described later, the membership dropped drastically. In 1926, there were 7,600 members; in 1927, 8,200; in early 1929, 9,300.[5]

The predominance of immigrants in the membership of the twenties was not simply a reflection of the make-up of the Socialist Party from which the Communists had emerged, for it was only in early 1919 that, for the first time, a majority of the Socialist Party was in the foreign-language federations (53 per cent in April 1919). By contrast, only 10 per cent of the Workers Party in 1922 was in the "English Section," as it was officially called; only 8 per cent in 1923; 11 per cent in 1924; 14 per cent in 1925.[6] Then the foreign-language federations in the Workers Party were abolished, though this move did not lead to any great increase in the nonimmigrant membership of the party. We thus have a problem of "selective recruitment" from the Socialist Party, or, rather, in view of the violence of the government raids and the additional rigors of life within the Communist movement in the early 1920's, of "selective survival." The foreign-language groups, or parts of them, survived to become members of the new party; the native elements and the more assimilated immigrants fell away.

Just as the foreign-language federations of the Socialist Party included only part of its foreign-born element, the same was true for the Communist parties and the Workers Party. Only those immigrant workers who habitually used a foreign language, who could not speak or were not at home in English, were members of foreign-language federations.[7]

These language groups or "language sections" varied enormously in size, in influence within the party, and in influence within their own ethnic communities. The first seven language federations of the Communist Party were those that had been expelled from the Socialist Party for adherence to the Left Wing in May 1919. They were made up of members from the Russian, Lettish, Lithuanian, Hungarian, Ukrainian, South Slavic, and Polish federations. They had contained more than 20,000 members, perhaps as many as 30,000.[8] The Russian Federation had been credited with 8,000 members in May, the Ukrainian with 4,000, the South Slavic with 3,000, the Lithuanian with 6,000, and the Lettish with 2,000. The Polish and Hungarian federations were probably smaller.[9] The Estonian federation was claimed by the Communist Party at its convention in September 1919,[10] and new Jewish and German federations were organized within the party after the convention.[11] In December 1920, most of the Finnish Federation withdrew from the Socialist Party. The Bohemian (Czecho-Slovak) Federation withdrew in August 1921, and the Jewish Federation in September 1921.[12] By 1925, the Workers Party included, in addition to members of all these groups, Armenian, Bulgarian, Greek, Italian, Romanian, and Scandinavian groups. There were thus eighteen organized foreign-language groups in addition to the English Section.[13]

The Finnish Section of the party was consistently the largest, with more than 6,400 members in 1925. The South Slavic (Yugoslav) Section had been second in size in 1922 and 1923, but was third in 1924 and 1925, with a little more than 1,000 members throughout the period. The Jewish Section had been third in size in 1922 and 1923, but moved to second in 1924 and 1925, with a membership that rose during this period from just under a thousand to almost 1,500. Fourth place in 1925, and for the two preceding years, was held by the Russian Section, with almost 900 members. Fifth, sixth, and seventh were the Lithuanian Section, with about 800 members, the Ukrainian, with about 600 members, and the Hungarian, with about 500 members. The English Section then had about 2,300 members. It had almost doubled since 1923—a much greater percentage

TABLE I · MEMBERSHIP IN FOREIGN-LANGUAGE SECTIONS OF WORKERS PARTY 1922—25 (*Yearly Averages*)

	1922 (*March through December*)	1923	1924	1925 (*January through June*)
Armenian	——	59	61	132
Czecho-Slovak	169	431	353	295
Esthonian	42	73	73	70
Finnish	5,846	6,583	7,099	6,410
German	463	461	442	350
Greek	88	142	203	256
Hungarian	313	374	469	509
Italian	138	412	581	331
Jewish	975	1,055	1,368	1,447
Lettish	597	417	443	434
Lithuanian	677	929	901	815
Polish	110	210	165	121
Roumanian	——	81	65	47
Russian	379	959	941	870
Scandinavian	33	259	248	211
South Slavic	1,077	1,158	1,290	1,109
Slovenian	——	——	——	14
Ukrainian	87	623	781	622
English	1,269	1,169	1,906	2,282
Total	12,058	15,395	17,377	16,325

Source: This table is from the unpublished doctoral thesis of Francis X. Sutton, "The Radical Marxist" (Harvard University, 1950). It is based on Workers (Communist) Party of America, *The 4th National Convention* (Chicago: Daily Worker Publishing Co., 1925), pp. 27-37.

of increase than any of the major foreign-language federations (see Table I).

But what did this membership composition mean for the party? How did it affect its activities, its public image, its ability to make an impact on the American scene? These are complicated questions, and statistics are only a partial guide to answering them.

To begin with, the social composition of the party—that is, the immigrant predominance—was viewed by the party itself throughout the twenties as one of its chief problems. During this period, the Comintern directed a steady stream of analyses, directives, and criticisms to the American party. These were based on the reports of Communists from America on official and unofficial business, which supplemented a steady stream of written reports. Almost all the major directives of the Comintern expressed serious concern with the problem of the party's composition. Clearly, a party that was made up of non-English-speaking elements in such large proportions would be limited in its impact on the American working class. It is true that the American working class was largely foreign-born. As Louis Fraina pointed out to the Second Congress of the Communist International in 1920, ". . . these unorganized and unskilled laborers are in a great majority of cases foreigners, amounting, in fact, to about 60 per cent of the industrial proletariat." [14] And yet, an American Communist Party had at least to be able to conduct its work, or a good part of it, in the English language. And one or two thousand English Section members were not enough for this task.

The first important message from the Comintern to American Communists, published in the party organ on August 15, 1920, sounds the note that was to be repeated often in the next ten years: The party must be an American party.

The party must not be a conglomerate of independent, autonomous "language federations." The federations have played an important historical part in the American Socialist Movement. . . . But now, with the rapid development of the class struggle, and when the American proletariat is faced with an extremely complicated problem, the language federations will only be in a position to fulfill their duty if they amalgamate as closely as possible with the organizations of the American workers.[15]

The language federations were separately organized, collected their own dues, ran their own newspapers. Despite this apparent independence, the complaint of the Comintern about the language-federation form of organization was not that the federations actively opposed party policies; it was, rather, that they formed an obstacle to the most complete deployment of party resources, because of their inability to reach out to other groups, in particular, to the native-born working class.

This, for example, is part of the import of the statement adopted after the Fourth Comintern Congress, held in Moscow during November and December of 1922:

The immigrants, including Communists, who have migrated to America from Europe, play an important part in the American Labor movement. But it must not be for the moment forgotten that the most important task is to arouse the American-born workers out of their lethargy. The Party must systematically and willingly assist American-born workers, whenever the opportunity offers, to play a leading part in the movement. The Communist immigrants have brought many virtues with them to America, self-sacrifice, revolutionary courage, etc. At the same time, however, their greatest weakness lies in the fact that they desire to apply the experience they have acquired in the various countries of Europe, mechanically to American conditions.[16]

At this time, the party had no daily newspaper. There existed a number of foreign-language Communist dailies, either acquired with the federations that had split from the Socialists or newly founded, but the official English-language publications appeared weekly or less often. At the Third Comintern Congress, during June and July of 1921, Lenin had emphasized to American delegates the importance of establishing a daily in English.[17] On August 23, 1923, the campaign for a *Daily Worker* was launched with a message from Gregory Zinoviev, chairman of the Communist International. Again, while complimenting the foreign Communists for their revolutionary vigor, the Comintern expressed its concern over the social composition of the American party. Zinoviev wrote:

The composition of the Workers Party with its eighteen language federations is unique among the parties of the Communist Internationale. Although these federations might act as a hindrance to revolutionary work, they, on the other hand, allow the Workers Party to come into direct contact with the great mass of foreign-born workers, who are the most exploited in the country. The Workers Party has, we think, solved the question of language federations in a satisfactory way, in that it regards the federations merely as propaganda sections of the party. . . .

The Communist Internationale notes with satisfaction also that several of the language federations have good, militant organs in their language whereby they are able to reach wide masses of workers. . . . It is a most deplorable fact that against some 10 foreign-language communist dailies there is not a single English communist daily in America. Every comrade whose heart beats for the sake of communism must and certainly does deplore this fact and realizes that until the workers party has at least one English daily with a wide circulation it will not be able to reach sufficiently wide masses of the American proletariat.

Comrades of the language federation!

The question of an English daily in the United States is as much your question as that of the English-speaking comrades. In fact it is more your problem, since you represent by far the major part of the Workers Party. . . .[18]

Quotas were laid upon the foreign-language federations according to their size to raise the necessary sums. When the Third National Convention of the Workers Party met on December 30, 1923, a few months after Zinoviev's appeal, $73,000 of the $100,000 needed to launch the newspaper had been raised.[19] When, shortly after the convention, Israel Amter announced in the international organ of the Comintern, *Inprecorr,* that the $100,000 had been raised, he spoke of what a great achievement this was for "a party of 22,000 members, of whom no more than 3,000 are English-speaking." [20] Amter exaggerated, for the benefit of the world movement, the size of the party, but he admitted that English speakers formed only a seventh of the party.

The next major move in the effort to adapt the party to the great need of reaching English-speaking workers was a radical reorganization, again carried out under Comintern directives.

In Moscow, the Communist International was being forged into a more disciplined, centralized, and monolithic organization, capable of responding to orders as effectively as a military body. The steps in the creation of such an organization were called "Bolshevization." Bolshevization was designed to expunge the last remnants of Socialist and Social Democratic ways of acting and thinking from the new Communist parties. For most Communist parties, this meant reorganization. The party was no longer to be based on territorial units, as were other parties designed to win elections, whose subordinate bodies followed the lines of electoral units. It was now to reflect the strategic distribution of power in a country, and its primary units were to be based on factories, mines, and other work places, and, on a larger scale, on industrial areas. Bolshevization also meant the addition of training courses for Communists, and the institution of a more severe discipline and control throughout the party.

For the American party, Bolshevization involved not only this, but also an attempt to overcome the inevitable effects of the division into language groups. If the Communist Party was to be truly "Bolshevik," responding as one man to orders, then not only must factions be eliminated, not only must organization reflect the "battle-plan" of the party (that is to say, its concentration on the key economic facilities), but all incidental divisions must be eliminated. Division into language units meant that, in some industries, Communists belonging to different language groups did not meet with each other or act with each other, and perhaps also distrusted each other. Bolshevization meant shifting the orientation of the average member from his ethnic group to his working group. As a member of an ethnic group—even if it were a Communist one—he read a foreign-language newspaper, was interested in events in the home country, and was involved in social relations with other fellow-language members. Bolshevization would take such a Communist and force him to "turn his face to the factory," where he would be made to fraternize with other Communists, and, hopefully, even with fellow workers who were not Communists and did not belong to any ethnic group. This was a peculiarly difficult task, and from 1925 to the end of the decade was the chief organizational problem of the Communist Party.

Bolshevization was inevitably to be a far more traumatic experience for the American party, then, than for more homogeneous parties. For these others, it meant shifting from a territorial base of organization to a factory base. For the American party, the wrench was a double one: from a territorial to an economic-functional base of organization, and from units based on language to units comprising members of various language groups.[21]

Bolshevization was the chief point on the agenda of an important meeting of the Communist International in Moscow in March and April 1925. It laid down the rule: "The principal and fundamental organizational form of every Bolshevik Party is the factory Party nucleus (the group of party members within a factory). The old principle of organization borrowed from the Social Democrats, according to which the Party is constructed on the basis of constituencies, convenient for parliamentary elections, is not acceptable to Communists." [22] And this principle was then spelled out for each party. The "Theses on the Bolshevization of the Parties of the Comintern" asserts that for America:

1) More intensive work must be conducted in the trade unions, and better organization of our influence on them (Communist fractions).

2) Fusion of all national groups of the Party into a real homogeneous party.

3) Greater attention to be paid to agitation connected with everyday conditions of working class life (application of united-front tactic).[23]

The necessary organizational steps were spelled out more fully in the "Resolution on the American Question." It said: "The organizational structure of the Party still lacks to a considerable extent the necessary cohesion. This is to be improved primarily by systematic, thorough concentration of the Party members of the different nationalities in centralized organizations. The formation of international branches [that is to say, those including all ethnic groups and "Americans," too] and factory nuclei is therefore on this account the most urgent organizational task of the Party." It is further specified: ". . . in every single trade union organization Party members must be organized in a Communist Fraction and must act unitedly on every question. . . ." [24] The necessary first step for the organization of such units and fractions was to break down the walls between the federations.

At the same 1925 meeting of the Comintern, James Cannon, one of the leaders of the party, and later the founder of American Trotskyism, gave an even soberer picture of the social composition of the American party than had Amter a year before. Cannon said:

We have a large proletariat in America, but the Party has only 20,000 members [again an exaggeration if official figures of dues-paying members are taken], of which only 2,000 are in English-speaking organizations [a more precise statement than Amter's, previously quoted]. . . . Our main difficulties are (1) we are a small party in a big industrial country; [25] (2) the trade union movement is very weak; (3) our party is divided into foreign language groups, each with its own national apparatus, and each tending toward specializing in the problems peculiar to the group. The language federation form of organization is absolutely incompatible with a Bolshevist organization. We must have a centralized form of organization, or we will never be a Bolshevist Party.[26]

Shortly thereafter, in August 1925, the Fourth Convention of the Workers Party met, and the party was reorganized to conform to the decisions of the Comintern. A new constitution was adopted—a step that generally marks a major turning point in the history of the party—and a new place was worked out for the foreign-language members. The previous constitution of the Workers Party had provided for branches, which could consist (and in most cases did) of members speaking a common foreign language and belonging to a language section; for "city central committees," consisting of two or more branches in a city or locality (a heritage from the old Socialist Party form of organization); and for "districts," large areas formed on the basis of a combination of economic and geographical considerations. The district tended to be a major industrial center with the area around it. Thus, the areas around New York, Philadelphia, Boston, Cleveland, Detroit, Pittsburgh, and Chicago formed districts.

The new, Bolshevized form of organization decreed that the basic unit was now either a "shop nucleus," composed of members in the same place of employment, or a "street nucleus," also called an "international branch," composed of members in the same neighborhood who were not regularly employed, presumably, or not employed in an enterprise where there were enough Communists to form a nucleus. There was no provision at all for language branches. The nuclei were grouped into sections, and, in large cities, subsections, directed by city executive committees. The district was retained as the largest basis of division. In the largest districts, there were also to be subdistricts.

The new form of organization that was now devised for the foreign-language work is described in Article 16, on "Language Fractions."

The term "fraction" is a crucial one in Communist organizational literature. It refers to the organization of Communist Party members working within a nonparty organization—trade union, benevolent society, cultural club, or other group. They are expected to organize into a fraction to maximize their impact, for whatever ends the party decrees, on the organization of which they are members. In the 1925 constitution, the term "fraction" was also applied somewhat confusingly to the members of a single foreign-language group *within* the party. They were to form a fraction within the party to control the work of the fractions within the nonparty organizations of that ethnic group. This usage of fraction for a specialized group within the party did not become common. Members in nonparty organizations continued to be called "fractions," but the foreign-language members within the party with a special interest in foreign-language work were organized into "sections" or "bureaus." With this single qualification as to the subsequent usage of the term "fraction," the 1925 constitution, in its prescriptions for the foreign-language members, gives a good picture of the way foreign-language work was to be henceforth carried on:

Section 1: All members of the Party now members of language branches must become members in either shop nuclei or international branches in the reorganization of the Party on the basis of this constitution, in order to retain their membership in the party.

Section 2: The former members of the language sections of the Party, in addition to their membership in the Party, through affiliation with the shop nuclei or international branch, shall form language fractions.

Section 3: The language fraction shall consist of all the members of the Party who speak a certain language, who are members of a subsection, section, or city organization of the Party. The units of the language fraction should be formed on the basis of the most efficient method of working among their particular language group. . . .

Section 7: The language fraction is an auxiliary organization of the Party for work among a particular language group. Only Party members who are affiliated to the shop nuclei or the street nuclei (international branches) and pay dues to the basic units of the Party, can be members of the language fraction of the Party. The language fraction of the Party does not collect dues, but may, with the consent of the Central Executive Committee, carry on special campaigns among their language groups for funds to carry on the work of the language fraction. . . .

Section 8: It is the work of the language fraction to carry on agitation, propaganda, and organization work among the working masses of its language group. The language fraction must also organize fractions of party members in the fraternal and benevolent organizations of its language group, as provided in the section of this constitution dealing with the organizational question [this requires party members in all organizations to form fractions], and carry on a systematic campaign to establish Communist influence and bring these organizations under the influence of the party, ideologically and organizationally. . . .[27]

This was an ideal picture of a Bolshevik party, of trained and dedicated professional revolutionaries capable of dominating large "mass" organizations. But in many cases the ideal became reality.

The form of organization thus decreed was carried out, with radical consequences for the party. There was a great drop in membership, for a good number of the members of the language groups were not material for Bolshevization. They belonged to language groups for the same reasons (at least in part) that other members of their ethnic group belonged to other organizations, and the attempt to transform them into single-minded soldiers of the revolution, to force them into association for purposes of political work with members of other groups, involved too strenuous an adjustment. This, at any rate, was the judgment of the party leaders. The losses from the reorganization were estimated by Jay Lovestone in 1927 to be fully one half of the party. The membership dropped from 14,037 in September 1925 to 7,215 in October 1925.[28]

Part of this enormous drop could be ascribed to a change in dues collection carried out at the same time as the reorganization. Previously, husband and wife were both considered members on the basis of a single dues payment. After 1925, every individual had to pay full dues for membership. The dual form of membership was probably more popular in the language federations, with their stronger social features, than in the English Section. Lovestone estimated the drop in membership from this cause at between 3,000 and 4,500. Even taking the largest estimate of reduction in membership from this cause, one finds almost 3,000 members lost because of other aspects of the re-organization—specifically, the abandonment of the foreign-language branch as the basic unit of organization.[29]

It was only after 1925, after the Comintern had decreed and the party had acted, that the leaders began to explain the weak-nesses inherent in the language-federation form of organiza-tion. This is presumably in line with the paradoxical dictum "The party never makes a mistake, but it always corrects its errors." It is characteristic of work with Communist literature that errors are "exposed" only after they have been completely "corrected." From some of the statements of party leaders ac-companying and following the reorganization, some light may be gained on the role of the foreign-language groups in the party. One interesting statement is that of the leader of the party, Charles Ruthenberg, writing in the *Workers Monthly,* in Oc-tober 1925:

All the language federations in the Socialist Party had been to a large degree national social organizations. Those language federa-tions which joined the Communist Party in 1919 lost through the government persecutions the major part of the element of its mem-bership which had joined them as social organizations. At least two-thirds of the membership of the federations which had joined the Communist Party in 1919 dropped out of the Party, leaving . . . only the conscious Communist elements.

This was not true of the Finnish Federation, the German Federa-tion, part of the Jewish Federation, the Czecho-Slovak Federation, and the Scandinavian Federation, all of which came into the Party only after the formation of the Workers Party. This group of the membership was still strongly under the influence of the Socialist traditions. . . .

[This] was particularly true of the Finnish Federation which com-posed at least one-third of the membership of our Party.

At the third National Convention, the Foster group . . . secured a majority of the national convention of the Party through the
support of the right-wing sectarian elements described above. . . .

Ruthenberg goes on to say of the Fourth Convention: "It was
exactly those elements which are the right-wing of our Party,
the Finnish Federation, the Czecho-Slovak Federation, the
Scandinavian Federation, part of the Jewish Federation, which
formed the basis of the Foster Group in the [Fourth] National
Convention." [30]

The attempt in this statement to give a Right Wing base to
the Foster faction, whose differences from the Ruthenberg faction can scarcely be described in terms of Right or Left, must
be discounted. But the point that social life was important for
the language groups is certainly valid. The ingenious attempt to
suggest that social life was more important for some language
groups (those that supported Foster) than others must also be
discounted. It was probably equally important for all.

Another party leader, Martin Abern, writing in 1926, pointed
out that attendance at meetings in the language units "had been
very low, often only 15, 20, 25 per cent; in the English branches
the attendance was from 50 per cent upwards. In the shop and
street nuclei a mean has already been reached averaging higher
than in the old form of organization." [31] Jack Stachel, writing
in 1929, also commented on the slackness of the foreign-born
members in participation in party work. "I remember the time
when we had in 1925 out of 1,100 Finnish members in New
York only 66 participating in elections in the units." (He was
referring to elections for higher party officers.) [32]

There is also some evidence that the language sections were
less energetic in recruiting than the English Section. Thus, in
1922, 45 per cent of the new members that came into the party
were recruited by the English Section, which formed only 10

per cent of the party during that year. In 1923, 55 per cent of the new members were recruited into the English Section, which that year formed but 8 per cent of the party. In 1924, 62 per cent came into the English Section, which in that year made up 11 per cent of the party. And for the first half of 1925, the English Section brought in no less than 72 per cent of the new members. And yet at the end of this period, the English Section accounted for only 14 per cent of the membership.[33]

While the English Section was the heaviest recruiter, it also lost the largest proportion of its recruits. It is fair to say that the English Section both gained many more and lost many more members than the foreign-language sections, which gained fewer and yet held those few they gained. The English Section acted much like the Communist Party of the thirties, with its great "fluctuation" (see Chapter IV); the foreign-language sections acted more like benevolent societies, in that their membership was stable.

In general, then, it may be said that a good part of the life of the party as a political organism was concentrated in the small English Section, while the language units tended to form a more passive periphery, supplying money and manpower.

Whatever the weaknesses introduced into the party by the heavy proportion of members of foreign birth, it was inevitable that these weaknesses should in large measure persist for years to come. Reorganization might be decreed from on top, and in a measure carried through, but the social forms of an organization, even a Communist Party, are rather resistant. On occasion, optimistic reports were turned in to the Comintern. One interesting report on the progress of the reorganization emphasizes the "assimilation" of the immigrants:

Three months after the 4th Convention [of the party, in 1925] the reorganization was declared to be 70% complete. . . .

. . . Most important is the great increase of forces released by the reorganization for regular party work: hundreds of comrades have been surprised to find that they have a sufficient command of English to take on active functions in the regular units and this has strengthened the ranks of lower unit functionaries. The record breaking attendance at classes in the English language conducted in every Party school, the holding of teachers conferences, etc., is the main factor in the "Americanization" process now going on in the Party.[34]

Inevitably, some of the brighter spots—and there were bright spots—of reorganization were selected for comment. The Political Committee minutes for January 14, 1927, have a report on the Ukrainian group, which lost fully two thirds of its members in the reorganization, yet still remained one of the stronger groups.[35]

But if the technical problem of reorganization was successfully managed, it was much harder to attain its objective: the redirection of the party efforts of immigrant members so that they co-operated with fellow Communists in their industries and work places. The valuable internal publication, the *Party Organizer,* which began publication in April 1927, gives a more realistic picture of the situation than the report to the Comintern. At the very time the Comintern report was published, an article by Ellis Paterson asked, "Are there Language Fractions or Sections in our Party?" It was introduced by an editor's note: "Comrade Paterson's article is a very timely one. The point of view he expresses is absolutely correct. This is the line of our Party. Certain exceptions are made from time to time in this transition stage because of the difficulties arising out of crisis with our language press etc. Comrade Paterson is correct in his warning that these 'transition' stages are too prolonged. . . ." And Comrade Paterson goes on to assert: *"There must not be any fractions in a Communist Party, not even language fractions.*

*There are fractions of Party members in non-party language or-
ganizations,* but there must not be language fractions IN the
Party. . . . There ought not to be democratic gatherings of
all comrades of a language group belonging to the Party in a
certain locality." [36]

In the study of ancient and medieval heresies, the truth may
be discovered by studying the attacks and admonitions of the
dominant orthodoxy. So, too, the truth about the Communist
Party may be discovered in the same way. Clearly, the foreign-
language comrades continued to meet as separate fractions
within the party, to gather together, not for factional purposes,
for that would have been known, but for social purposes. Even
this was, of course, a distraction of energy that could have gone
into party work, and was therefore attacked.

A specific account was given in the *Party Organizer* in 1928
of the situation in the East Pennsylvania coal fields, where the
party had always had some strength through its language groups.
The editor introduced the article by pointing out the lesson:
"Although the Party reorganization was carried through in the
fall of 1925 up to the time Comrade Gardos was elected a Sub-
district organizer of the Anthracite, not a single mine nucleus
was organized. In a period of less than three months Comrade
Gardos has been successful in forming six mine nuclei. . . ."

Comrade Gardos wrote:

Not very long ago, our Party in the Anthracite Sub-district showed
a picture of small language units hardly changed by reorganization
with some exceptions. The comrades did not participate in the
struggles of the workers. They might have been members of the
same mine, belonging to the same local union without even noticing
it. Party work consisted mostly of language affairs for the party
paper, work in the [benevolent] society, isolated from the rest of
the miners.[37]

If the anthracite subdistrict was a bright spot in 1928, show-ing how federationism and ethnic exclusiveness could be over-come, the danger of backsliding was never far behind. Less than two years later, another organizer in the same district was complaining about the foreign-language fraternal organizations: they would not work among the miners and would not rent their fraternal halls to the party because they were afraid to lose "their licenses to sell booze." [38] (How they managed to get such licenses during Prohibition is not clear, but perhaps the reference is to informal arrangements with the local authorities.) In February 1930, four and a half years after reorganization, the *Party Organizer* reported: "In some sections of our largest district [this means New York] we still have only 'language branches' of the party. . . . It must be made clear once and for all in our Party that there are only two forms of units in a Communist Party: shop nuclei and street nuclei." [39]

The Comintern continued to speak out on "federationism" in the late twenties. But its directives and analyses had a some-what different tone from those of the earlier period. It was now increasingly concerned with struggles between the Lovestoneite and the Fosterite groups. It now saw (or professed to see) a major cause of this factionalism in the numerical predominance of foreign-born members. Thus, in 1927 it declared:

The objective difficulties, the weaknesses of the Workers (Com-munist) Party * and its inadequate contact with the masses of native workers are factors complicating the inner situation of the Workers (Communist) Party. An insufficiently strong Party life, as a result of an insufficient mass basis, and the inadequate contact of many members of the former language groups with the specific problems

* This is the name the party took at the time of the 1925 reorganiza-tion. In 1929, it became simply the Communist Party of the United States of America.

of the class struggle in the United States favour the development of groups and factional struggles, the existence and intensity of which we seek in vain to explain by serious differences of principle.[40]

The important Open Letter of March 1, 1929, addressed to the Sixth Convention of the party, also asserted that there was a relationship between the immigrant composition and factionalism:

The Workers (Communist) Party of America has been for many years an organization of foreign workers not much connected with the political life of the country. Owing to this immigrant exclusiveness two leading groups arose, took shape and became consolidated within the Party. For six years an almost uninterrupted struggle for supremacy in the Party has been going on between them.[41]

But within a few months, the factionalism within the party was to be overcome by the expulsion of the Lovestoneite leadership on the orders of the Comintern. The fact that only a handful of members followed it out of the party it had so recently controlled, and that no major foreign-language group or newspaper went with it, suggests that the Comintern was in error in its analysis: the foreign-language groups played no independent role in the factionalism of the twenties.

The same Sixth Convention to which this Open Letter was addressed also heard a detailed organizational report from Jack Stachel. It gave a full picture of the composition of the party membership at the time, and suggested the degree to which a cadre of English-speaking members had already been built up. Stachel said: "If you study our membership on the basis of language composition you will find that on the basis of about 14,000 or 13,000 members [fully paid-up members were 9,300] about 8,000 or 9,000 are registered in the various languages." [42]

Presumably, then, about 5,000 members were not registered with any language group—a number perhaps twice the size of the English-speaking group on the eve of reorganization. But many of these were, nevertheless, foreign-born members. Stachel gave the following proportion of "American" workers, as he called them, in various districts: In the Pittsburgh District, 95 out of 550 members were native-born; in Minnesota, 50 out of 850; in the Kansas City District, 86 out of 278; in the Philadelphia District, 50 out of 481; and in Cleveland, 70 out of 412. Of these 2,571 members in five representative districts, a sizable proportion of the party, about 88 per cent were foreign-born.[43]

Through the twenties, the party leaders, Comintern and native, emphasized only the weaknesses created in the movement by the predominance of foreign-language members. Indeed, the problems were severe.

To begin with, only a few party workers capable of using English and working among the mixed American working class were available, even fewer than the party rolls suggested. Here is one striking example of this scarcity of English-speaking and English-using manpower: One of the important world campaigns of the late twenties was the effort to establish shop papers. This was part of the whole effort to Bolshevize, to "root the party in the factories and among the heavy industrial workers." Actually, the American party was one of the more successful ones in the establishing of shop newspapers. When Ossip Piatnitsky, head of the Organization Department of the Comintern, discussed shop papers in a report on the world movement in 1928, his first example was from America, where the *Ford Worker,* with a circulation of 20,000 to 22,000 copies, was by far the most successful shop paper in the world movement.[44] An insight into how this success was achieved can be found in the *Party Organizer* of the same year. It is there reported about one party nucleus in Detroit: "This nucleus, in line with the new policy of the District, has taken over its own factory paper. Formerly one comrade in Detroit wrote all the factory papers (with the exception of the *Ford Worker*)." [45]

This policy of having an outsider who knew English write the shop paper was characteristic. In 1930, the *Party Organizer* reported: "It may be necessary for comrades not members of the nucleus, to help in writing the paper, due to insufficient command of English language by the members, but when the paper is ready to be issued, it is absolutely imperative that the members of the nucleus go over every bit of material and check up on the facts." [46] Apparently some peculiar things had found their way into shop papers ostensibly issuing from within the party unit at a plant.

A Boston organizer reported at the Organization Conference in 1930: "We had great difficulties in issuing shop papers because most of our members could not write English . . . we overcame this by having them write the articles in their own languages and having them translated." [47]

The problems caused by the scarcity of members competent in English extended, of course, beyond that of issuing shop papers. The nucleus in Detroit that had adopted the policy of issuing its own newspaper was described earlier in the report as being composed as follows: "The nucleus in question has twenty-five members. . . . The factory employs 15,000 workers. Our comrades are scattered through different departments. Half of them speak English with difficulty. Some not at all." [48] The difficulties of making an impact on this plant or on the country as a whole can easily be imagined. The image of the Communist as an outlandish foreigner, so common in America, is derived from the reality of the twenties.

This situation required the party to become an Americanizing agency. The report to the Comintern in 1928 spoke of the party's English classes (always popular). In addition, it encouraged members to use their broken English.

"Some comrades," a Jewish member from Philadelphia wrote in 1931, "say they cannot speak English and therefore they cannot be useful in organizing block committees and other organization activities. This is merely an excuse." He described how he went about organizing a block committee for the defense of the Scottsboro boys: "When the workers came to the door and asked what we wanted we didn't have to speak to him in a particular fancy language to explain what we came for." And afterward, at the meeting: "I explained to them in my broken English the purpose in organizing the block committees." [49]

However, it was not only the incapacity of the foreign-born members to conduct propaganda and organization work in English that hampered the party in the use of this manpower. There was also considerable resistance to moving outside an ethnic community to participate in the larger struggle. Indeed, there was considerable resistance to letting anyone from the larger community get into the party. This complaint about the exclusiveness of the foreign-language members, an exclusiveness based either on fear of outsiders or on the greater ease of working within their own community, was voiced again and again in the Organization Conference of 1930:

Flint: ". . . we practically have a foreign party—when we began to do real activity—they were afraid that the American workers were spies. . . ." (Of course, the American workers had good grounds to think the same of them!)

Pontiac: ". . . in Pontiac we had a party of almost all foreigners." They were afraid to expose themselves and conducted no activity.

Upstate New York: "Whenever an American joins the Party

there is open opposition that he is a spy. Five or six comrades suspended from the Party—American comrades, and everyone was suspected of being a spy and when I came there and started my work, they nearly accused me of a spy because I took the part of these comrades."

Chicago: ". . . the reason they [the shop nuclei] are dead is because they are mostly composed of foreign-born comrades who are afraid of American workers."

Minnesota: Again, the fear of spies hampers the party work.

Eastern Pennsylvania: The old members drive away the new. "In our district before we can make any headway we will have to reorganize from the bottom." [50]

Thus the foreign-language members were unable to engage in certain kinds of work for the party, and they often resisted the introduction of members who might. Did they also resist the party out of some special interest, a unique ideological bent, a tendency to ally themselves with some minority faction? A student of the theory of organization might expect that the foreign-language groups would serve as independent centers of power, for, free in some measure from central party control, they could have become a base for, or a screen to protect, factional activities. Yet they seem to have played almost no role in this respect. The factional struggles of the twenties were conducted among the leaders at the party center, and these leaders all operated within the English Section, though drawing support at one time or another from different ethnic groups. (An example of this is Ruthenberg's comment on Foster's support, quoted earlier.) But the ethnic groups did not form independent powers after the first few years, when Russian leaders played some role in party affairs.[51] There were almost no major party leaders drawn from the language federations. The Jewish Federation was perhaps the sole exception in this respect. Leaders in this group did play a role in central party affairs. But interestingly enough, they seem to have played this role not as leaders of a separate base of strength—the Jewish Federation—but in their capacity as experts on Bolshevik ideology, owing to their knowledge of Russian and their firsthand acquaintance with Russian Communist writings.[52]

Why did the federations play so little role as a separate base of strength? In part, this was owing to the strongly centralized party that was being built up even while the language federations led a separate existence. Thus, the party early became the owner of the foreign-language newspapers. It reported to the Third Convention, held in December 1923 and January 1924: "The C.E.C. [Central Executive Committee], following the policy of the last convention that the Party press should come under the centralized ownership of the Party during the year, took over the ownership of the [Yiddish] *Freiheit* and the [Hungarian] *Elore.* The *Freiheit,* since the beginning of May, has been under the direct management of the C.E.C." [53]

Organizational measures helped secure for the center control over the language groups. But more important than any organizational measures was the power of the Bolshevik myth. The party leaders spoke for the party, the party stood for the Communist International, and the International's authority was absolute. Those who spoke for the center—the Russian leaders who had carried through the successful revolution and ran the International—owned the individual Communist, regardless of what language he spoke or what newspaper he read. The party center, convention, or political committee gave orders to the federations—and, while these may have dragged their feet or organized some petty sabotage, when the issue was important, the party center was obeyed. Theoretically, it was possible for a newspaper editor or a language federation to resist, but by resistance they risked the privilege of remaining Communists, and this was a prospect from which Communists withdrew in horror. This is the only way to explain the fact that there were no breakaways of newspapers or organized language groups from the party.

This should not be surprising to a student of the Communist movement. It was not owing to his organizational astuteness alone that Stalin was able to throw the Lovestone group out of the party they apparently so solidly controlled in 1929. Astute he indeed was, but it is doubtful that he needed organizational measures to keep the American party loyal to the Comintern (that is, to himself). As he said to the American delegates in Moscow on May 14, 1929:

The group of Comrade Lovestone speaks and represents itself here in the name of the whole Party, in the name of 99 per cent of the Communist Party of America. . . . That is a bad manner, comrades of the American delegation. Let me remind you that Zinoviev and Trotsky also at one time played trumps with percentages, and assured everybody they had secured, or at any rate would secure, a 99 per cent majority in the ranks of the C.P.S.U. . . . You declare you have a certain majority in the American Communist Party, and that you will retain that majority under all circumstances. That is untrue, comrades of the American delegation, absolutely untrue. You had a majority because the American Communist Party until now regarded you as the determined supporters of the Communist International. And it was only because the Party regarded you as the friend of the Comintern that you had a majority in the ranks of the American Communist Party. But what will happen if the American workers learn that you intend to break the unity of the ranks of the Comintern and are thinking of conducting a fight against its executive bodies—that is the question, dear comrades? . . . you will find yourselves completely isolated if you attempt to start a fight against the decisions of the Presidium of the Executive Committee of the Comintern. You may be cerain of that dear Comrades.[54]

Had any foreign-language group raised the banner against the far less august leaders of the Communist Party of the United States, they would have been spoken to in the same way. And had they resisted the party as Lovestone resisted the Comintern, they would have led as small a proportion of their groups out of the Communist Party.

Nothing quite this dramatic ever occurred in the relations between the party center and the foreign-language groups. The party gave its orders and directives, and since the essence of being a Communist was to obey, they were generally obeyed. There were certainly problems in checking on publications in a score of languages, and such publications could get away with something less than the purest version of the party line for a while. But in the end, the center caught up.

All through the twenties, this control of the ethnic groups can be seen in operation, with relatively little friction. Some passages from the documents of this period will suggest the nature of the control.

From the Third Convention report, made at the beginning of 1923:

> The third convention instructs the incoming Central Executive Committee to continue in its efforts to establish a uniform press policy and action for all the Party press.
>
> The editors of the Federation papers are urged to pay close attention to the central organ of the Party and to the Press Service issued by the National Office and to take active part in all campaigns conducted by the party. The Federation Press should apply itself more than before with American conditions and not so much to European problems.
>
> The Federation Press must devote sufficient space to the clarification of the various policies and issues of the Party regardless of whether the editor agrees with the official stand of the Party or not.[55]

The Fourth National Convention, held in mid-1925, took a direct hand in disciplining a foreign-language newspaper editor:

The Convention considers that the further employment of Comrade Askeli as editor of [the Finnish] *Tyomies* is incompatible with the interests of our Party and its Bolshevization.

Therefore the convention instructs the Finnish comrades of Superior to remove at once Comrade Askeli from the staff of *Tyomies* and to replace him with a comrade who understands, accepts, and fights for the Communist line of our Party and the Communist International.[56]

In the minutes of the Political Committee for October 10, 1925, the Russian *Novy Mir,* which had requested permission to expand, is asked to explain how it will finance the expansion. In the minutes of June 27, 1928, the Polish *Trybuna Robotnicza* requested permission to suspend for a period of one month; permission was denied owing to the role it was expected to play among the miners in the immediate future.[57]

The report of the Organization Conference of 1930 contains many petty examples of ethnic groups falling afoul of the party line. In general, their errors consisted of being too "petty bourgeois," of being more interested in and affected by the problems and point of view of the ethnic community than the policy of the world Communist movement. The newspapers acted sometimes as ethnic community papers rather than Communist papers. The Polish newspaper was accused of printing an advertisement of a "religious fascist" organization. A Lithuanian paper had referred to a "social fascist" (which meant "social democrat" in the language of this period) as a progressive. The Czechoslovak newspaper had printed a picture of a millionaire's son (presumably in a favorable context). In the Macedonian paper there was not a word about the class struggle.[58]

These were venial sins, even though they did not escape the attention of strict Bolsheviks. Indeed, it was Moscow itself which had brought the attention of the American comrades to the mistake of the Lithuanian newspaper; [59] apparently, all the newspapers were being read closely there.

A more important kind of resistance offered by the ethnic community was represented by the case of the Lithuanian group in Chicago. The Communist leader in charge of language work described what happened at the Organization Conference of 1930:

> In the Lithuanian office where there was a fight against the moving of Negroes in this territory and when our comrades were called upon by the District to fight this the committee in the *Vilnis* [the Lithuanian newspaper] said this had nothing to do with them, which means that the *Vilnis* has nothing to do with the Party . . . we must understand the meaning of the Lithuanian comrades only from a commercial viewpoint. [Presumably they were afraid of losing readers and advertisements if they took the party position.] The first question with these comrades is money and then after that the line of the Party.[60]

Clarence Hathaway gave more details on this incident: "White chauvinism manifested itself sharply even among the leading comrades of the District. In Roseland, a section in which *Vilnis* is published, they organized the homeowners association to bar Negroes. . . ." The business manager of *Vilnis* refused to accept the instructions of the district committee. "The business manager had to be removed, the manager of the cooperative restaurant had to be removed."

The party was quite correct in seeing these as "petty bourgeois" manifestations, for they reflected the fact that many of the ethnic comrades were homeowners and members of a community. Thus, the problem of "white chauvinism" was a recurrent one. To quote Hathaway again: "In St. Louis the Jewish comrades there owned a hall right in the very center of the Negro neighborhood and when the Section Organizer proposed to call meetings of Negro workers in this hall they refused on the grounds that this would depreciate the value of the property." [61]

The most dramatic case of this kind of white chauvinism occurred in the Finnish community in New York, where August Yokinen was in 1931 "tried" before an audience of 1,500 for refusing to allow Negroes to enter a dance at the Finnish Hall.[62]

In this case, the party was more interested in the effect of this trial on the Negroes, for whom they were then making a strong drive, than in the virulence of white chauvinism in the ethnic communities. Yet in the Organization Conference discussions it does seem that the party leaders saw the ethnic comrades as less committed, less completely reliable Communists than the nonethnic members. And they were probably right: basic to the work with language groups, no matter how things were organized, no matter what kind of measures were taken to limit and control their independence, was the fact of another commitment, another allegiance, independent to some degree of commitment and allegiance to the party. And *any* commitment outside the party was a potential threat to Bolshevik discipline and obedience.

Sometimes this independent commitment gave rise to somewhat more serious deviations. There were problems of "nationalist ideology." The Jewish Bureau was called to task at the Organization Conference for its position on the Palestine affair— it had not been as violent in its attacks on Zionism as it should have been. There was also a problem about the schools maintained by a number of fractions—the Jewish, Ukrainian, and Czechoslovak: "They go along the old line of developing a national culture. They cannot understand that this school shall be a school of class struggle and that we use the language only to bring the children in this line." [63]

And yet, all these examples of petty-bourgeois resistance to the party line and nationalist deviation should not obscure the main point—that the deviations were minor, the resistance hardly visible. And the party was aware that the matter was not really serious. It appreciated that it itself contributed to the weakening of the language groups by drawing off their best comrades for other work. As a leader of this work said: "We must understand that these comrades are not only opportunist but terribly weak because the best elements of the language work become organizers of the Party." [64] And a Lithuanian comrade, explaining what happened in the white chauvinism fight in Chicago, pointed out that right in the middle of this fight one of the members involved was taken away and made a district organizer.[65]

These were the weaknesses introduced into the party, seen from the point of view of the party itself. Looking at the matter from a larger perspective, there is one important weakness obvious to the outside observer, but hardly mentioned in the party. That is the foreign image of the party in the United States. The Communist Party was necessarily seen as a foreign group because of the commitment to Russia, the open avowal of Russian leadership, the open publication and discussion of Comintern directives. But it was made even more "foreign" by the fact that such a large proportion of Communists were unacculturated immigrants. In a phase when Communism proudly and without compromise emphasized its international, revolutionary, and antipatriotic character, this was not likely to be seen as a drawback by Communists; but unquestionably it served to lessen the very limited impact of Communism on America in the 1920's.

However, the matter must now be looked at from a different perspective: What did the Communist Party gain as a result of this special social composition in the twenties? This was not something that was discussed in the party, and yet any objective consideration of the party and its problems in the twenties must come to the conclusion that it also gained a good deal from its foreign-language membership. The gains were three: The party gained money; it gained access to the industrial working class; it gained cadres, drawn from the foreign-language groups, which it was able to use effectively in the period of growth in the thirties.

The problem of how much money the Communist Party disposed of, and its sources, is a most interesting one. Benjamin Gitlow, one of the top leaders of the twenties, wrote, of 1927-28, "we spent on an average of a million dollars a year, of which the better half was raised right here in the United States." [66] Is this excessive? I do not think so. An official report for the year ending November 30, 1923, gives receipts of $138,000.[67] This was early in the history of the Workers Party, and would not include the money raised in special drives, such as the $100,000 to launch the *Daily Worker* raised in the latter part of 1923 and the early part of 1924, or the sums required to run various front operations, to maintain a dozen newspapers, many with heavy expenses, to run various local offices and local operations, and to run affiliated language organizations. In any case, great sums of money were necessary to run the party, and the foreign-language groups were one of the most important domestic sources for this money. Language groups might be assigned quotas to raise money for certain party purposes, as in the case of the *Daily Worker* campaign; money they had in hand might even be taken for party purposes. In the Political Committee minutes for October 13, 1926, an official of the Yiddish daily *Freiheit* "is instructed to turn over 35 per cent of the receipts from the *Freiheit* campaign in District 8 [Chicago] to the *Daily Worker*." [68] In 1930, the language fractions were expected to supply the money for a Southern newspaper. A number of speakers at the 1930 Organization Conference emphasized this point: "The establishment of a Southern paper," one said, "must go forward and the comrades of the language fractions who bear the primary responsibility of raising funds must develop ways and means of rallying foreign-born workers in this campaign." [69]

More important than the direct supply of funds for party purposes was the role of the language groups in supporting a large proportion of the party cadres. The Communist Party emphasizes the necessity of having the largest number of people working full time for the party. It is this feature of a Communist Party that makes so unrealistic the judgment of Communist strength by means of membership figures alone, for a Communist Party will have far more paid employees than other political groups and will be capable of mobilizing a much larger proportion of its membership for any given task. Just how many employees the Communist Party had during the twenties is hard to determine. Piatnitsky gave figures in 1928 for paid employees of a number of Communist parties, three larger and one smaller than the Communist Party of the United States. The Communist Party of Germany had almost 300 paid employees, that of France over 100, that of Czechoslovakia about 140, and that of Great Britain about 50. The American Communist Party certainly had many more than 50 paid employees. Members of the Central Executive Committee (nineteen according to the

1925 constitution; thirty-seven according to the 1929 constitution) to begin with were generally either in the employ of the party or of an organization controlled by it. (As Cannon wrote: "We decreed that no one could be a member of the Central Committee of the party unless he was a full-time professional party worker, or willing to become such at the call of the party." [70]) Each district had full-time employees, the number depending on the size, and there were about twenty districts organized in 1930. Gitlow, in an occupational breakdown of the party, said that in 1925, of 13,556 members, 2,000 were party functionaries.[71] This figure appears on the face of it incredible, yet if all the employees of trade unions, fronts, affiliated organizations, newspapers, and so on were included, we would not fall too far short of that figure.

The language groups played an important role in allowing a much higher proportion of the party membership to be full-time workers than the party resources alone would have allowed. People engaged in full-time or nearly full-time party work often drew their salaries from a language newspaper, a fraternal organization, or some other group. Max Silver, for example, who was engaged in party work in Chicago, Philadelphia, and Los Angeles in the late twenties and early thirties, got his salary as business manager of the Yiddish *Freiheit* in these cities, and he was employed by the *Freiheit* initially at the direct request of party authorities.[72] John Lautner's first party assignment, in June 1930, to work in Detroit as district secretary of the Hungarian Bureau (part of the Language Department under the Central Committee of the Communist Party), was a full-time job, for which he received a salary from the party, plus a percentage from subscriptions to the Hungarian newspaper.[73] The Political Committee minutes for 1928 contain a resolution calling for a central directory of all the available jobs in which party workers can be placed:

> All auxiliary organizations, language papers, *Daily Worker,* language bureaus, District Committees, should within one week after the receipt of these instructions supply the National Office with a list of employees, their functions, their salaries and should also indicate whether they are Party members or not. This should include technical workers as well as political workers.
>
> On the basis of these returns, the Polbureau should later consider the proposal to have some of the auxiliaries assume the salaries of some of the National Office employees.[74]

Another benefit brought to the Communist Party by the foreign-language groups was the access they provided to industrial workers. The industrial working class in America in the twenties, and in declining proportions in the thirties, was foreign-born: if the party was less "American" for being in such large measure an immigrant party, it was by the same token more "working-class." Small as it was, the party during the twenties was really a working-class organization. As Draper describes the situation:

> It appears from the imperfect official records that [at the end of 1923] possibly two-thirds to three-quarters of the party could be classified as "proletarian," a much larger percentage than it ever achieved in later years. In this early period the foreign-language federations gave a working-class character to the American Communist movement. . . . The Communist bid against John L. Lewis for power in the mine union was based on this foreign-language strength.[75]

At this time, 14 per cent of the party were metal workers, 12 per cent building workers, 10 per cent miners, 8 per cent clothing workers—sizable percentages in important industries. A registration of the membership of September 1924 shows about the same percentages in these four industries. A registration of May-July 1928 reflects an increase of needle-trade workers (up to 15 per cent of the membership), a decline of metal workers (to 8.5 per cent of the membership), and the maintenance of a sizable group of miners (12 per cent).[76]

Draper's judgment that the party's strong fight for control of the mineworkers' union was largely based on its foreign-language strength has already been quoted. William Z. Foster, in his official history of the party, suggests much the same thing.[77] In 1925, the Communists made a strong bid for control of the United Brotherhood of Carpenters and Joiners. This, according to a historian of Communist activities in American trade unions in the 1920's, "is the only union composed chiefly of native-born workers in which the influence of the Workers Party can be traced to an appreciable degree." But "the only local unions in which the Workers Party and the [Trade Union Educational] League have been able to gain a foothold are those composed almost entirely of foreign-born members, as local 376 in New York, or those in which the members are chiefly foreign-born." [78]

Within unions, the Communist strength was generally based on foreign-born workers, or else the membership of the unions was almost completely foreign-born (as was the case in the needle-trade unions of New York). Where the Communists led important strikes—that of the cloakmakers in New York in 1926, and of the textile workers in Passaic, New Jersey, the same year—they were largely strikes of foreign-born workers. Indeed, very likely the first major strike run by the party that was not a strike of immigrant workers was that of textile workers in Gastonia, North Carolina, in 1929. This was remarkable enough to be noted by William Z. Foster in his official history:

"The workers involved were almost entirely American-born, for several generations back." [79]

Since the party was "rooted" in the immigrant groups, it was by the same token "rooted" in the industrial working class. And the more perceptive party leaders realized this. Louis Fraina's remark at the beginning of the decade, at the Second Congress of the Comintern, that 60 per cent of the industrial proletariat were foreigners has previously been cited. At the end of the decade, Jack Stachel pointed out in his organization report to the Sixth Convention: "We face the fact that the working class of this country, in its national composition, consists of a majority of foreign born. For example, we find that 67% of the oil workers are foreign born, 62% of the packinghouse workers, 61% of the miners. We find textile workers over 60%, clothing workers also over 60%, steel workers over 60%. . . ." [80]

The party, then, was a working-class party; and it was a working-class party because the greater part of its membership came from certain immigrant communities.

The third and most important gain from its foreign-language membership was the cadre: trained, committed, disciplined Communists, at the disposal of the party, ready to work for it in whatever area and for whatever end the central leadership directed. This, in the end, is a chief goal of a Communist Party: the creation of Communists. What they will be used for depends on circumstances not in their hands: whether for revolution or reform, for war or peace, for overthrowing governments or supporting governments, for sabotaging industrial production or pressing for greater industrial production. Defeats and victories in any campaign are less important in themselves (next time, a totally different campaign may be required, for an opposite end) than for what the party extracts from the campaign: membership. And membership is important because only out of

members can be made, through schooling, training, and experience, cadres. The ultimate success or failure of the party, from
the time of Lenin, has been seen as dependent on cadres.

From this point of view, the period of foreign-language predominance may be considered a success: a powerful cadre
emerged that was to place its stamp, in subsequent decades, on
parts of the American social structure. In this sense, too, the
Communist Party was a peculiarly effective Americanizing de-
vice. It had to take immigrants and turn them into people who
could work with Americans of varied backgrounds, of different
classes.

The party was forced to work with immigrant material because it had so little other material. But by the thirties, many
Communists were emerging from within the ethnic subsections
of the party with varied abilities and skills. The Yorkville Unit
of the Harlem Section of the Communist Party can serve as an
example. Despite the reorganization of a year or two before, it
was, it appears, entirely Hungarian in composition. In effect,
many language units simply transformed themselves into "international units," and this was probably one of them. John Lautner, one of the highest placed Communists who gave information on the party in the period after 1930, described this unit,
the first he joined as a Communist, in testimony before the Subversive Activities Control Board in 1952:

At the time I joined that unit I recall the following members
of the Communist Party who were in that particular political department: Abe Markoff, who was known as the founder of the
Worker's School [and who was the chief figure in the development
of the Communist Party's system of internal training schools]; Louis
Bebrits, who at that time was one of the editorial board members
of the Hungarian Communist Party newspaper known as *Uj Elore*.
Today Bebrits . . . is Minister of Transport in the Hungarian Communist Government. A member of that unit was Dr. John Gyetvai,

who up until the time I left the Communist Party was Minister to Turkey representing the Hungarian Government. A member of that unit was John Szanto, who was treasurer of the Transport Workers International Union [and who also returned to Hungary to take an important job with the Hungarian government]; James Lusztig, who is an international representative of the United Electrical Workers Union; Louis Sass, who was a Party organizer for many years [and who was particularly important in building the powerful Northwest District of the party in the middle thirties]. . . . Louis Weinstock [a member of the National Committee of the party, and an important official of the Brotherhood of Painters] was also a member of this Yorkville Unit. At that time he was business manager of the . . . *Uj Elore*.[81]

All these men, and John Lautner himself, formed part of the cadre of the Communist Party during the thirties and forties. The mere listing of the jobs they held for the party would take many pages. Lautner himself, as has been said, first began work for the party as district secretary for the National Hungarian Bureau of the party in Detroit in 1930. Then he became editor of a weekly Hungarian Communist paper in Canada and secretary of the National Hungarian Bureau in the Canadian party; next went to the editorial board of *Uj Elore* and became district secretary for the National Hungarian Bureau in Cleveland. In 1933—still working within the language area, but now outside the Hungarian area—he was assigned by the New York District Language Department to East Harlem, to work with Spanish-speaking groups there. Later in 1933 came his first job outside the language area: he became section organizer for a newly formed section on the Upper West Side of Manhattan, running from 59th Street to 110th Street, from Central Park to the Hudson River. Since a section is the next area under a district, a section organizer holds an important position. In 1936, Lautner went to West Virginia as district organizer, and held that job until 1940. In 1941, he returned to New York to participate in an intensive national training school, lasting three months, full-time, for a handful of selected leaders. He then became national secretary of the Hungarian Bureau and a member of the National Language Department of the party. During this period he was also briefly secretary of the Hungarian Section of the International Workers Order (I.W.O.), the major fraternal organization of the party. He was drafted in 1942, and had an honorable army career which included writing and broadcasting propaganda to Hungary. After the war, he returned to work with the National Hungarian Bureau, then went on to special organizational jobs for New York County, particularly in connection with the reorganization of the party after the Browder Communist Political Association episode. In early 1947, he became head of the New York State Review Commission, and in 1948, he was made a member of the National Review Commission, the highest job he held in the party. These bodies were concerned with security, and served as the courts of the party, checking the credentials of members and reviewing expulsions.

The careers of the other men who came out of the Hungarian group in New York in 1926—Weinstock, Szanto, Lusztig—which may be traced in various Congressional hearings, are as extensive, and show the same pattern of movement from tasks within the Hungarian group to assignments in the general structure of the party, and (though this is lacking in Lautner's case) important posts in the labor movement.

Had the party had a different composition in the twenties, it would have created a cadre from different elements. But limited though it was by the predominance of recent immigrants, it did manage to create from them a powerful corps of Communist workers.

•

The strongest ethnic groups within the Communist Party, in the order of size of membership in 1925, were the Finnish, Jewish, South Slavic, Russian, Lithuanian, Ukrainian, and Hungarian. There is no more impressive demonstration of the stability of social patterns to be found than the constancy with which these seven groups maintained their positions as important ethnic groups within the Communist Party. Of the more than twenty nationalities among which there existed some kind of Communist organization (to those listed in Table I, might be added Albanians, Syrians, Bulgarians and Macedonians, Carpatho-Russians, Spanish, Japanese, Chinese, and Koreans, which at one time or another had Communist organizations of some kind),[82] these remained, for a period of about thirty-five years (from the middle of the twenties to the end of the fifties), the most important.

In 1925, the Communist Party published daily newspapers in seven languages in addition to English. They were Finnish, Yiddish, Russian, Lithuanian, Ukrainian, and Hungarian; the seventh was the German *Volkszeitung.*[83] There was as yet no Croatian daily, but the *Radnik* was appearing three times a week, and a few years later it was appearing daily. By that time, the German-language daily, which had been inherited from the Socialist Party, and which did not reflect any strong German Communist group in this country, was no longer appearing. The newspaper list for 1930 [84] showed at least one daily for each of the seven major foreign-language groups. In addition, there was then a Slovak daily. This pattern was to be maintained fairly steadily through the thirties and forties. In these eight groups, Communist organization and influence were generally strong enough to support a daily newspaper.

The consistency with which certain ethnic groups supplied supporters for the Communist Party, while others did not, is the first important datum in trying to understand the reasons for Communist strength (and weakness) in foreign-language groups in this country. It would seem on the face of it to rule out any explanation of Communist strength among the foreign-born workers in terms of conditions affecting them in general. To say that foreign-born workers generally worked under worse conditions than native-born workers is probably true. To say further that they felt a sense of resentment which might have led them more frequently than native-born workers to join a revolutionary party seems more questionable: the most responsible historians of immigration have felt that the foreign-born immigrant workers tended to be conservative, and supporters of American institutions.[85]

Beyond that, to explain the behavior of the tens of thousands of individuals who joined the Communist Party in terms of factors affecting millions in the immigrant working class would seem to be the worst sort of logical error. Nevertheless, it would be equally wrong to conclude that we are left with a multitude of individual experiences for which no general explanation can be given. While the membership of the Communist Party contained only a small fraction of the immigrant workers as a whole, it was a much more substantial fraction of *some* immigrant groups. In some groups, indeed, Communist influence was of major importance.

It would be convenient to have a simple measure of the strength of this influence in the different immigrant communities. One such measure—despite a variety of pitfalls in its use— would be the proportion of the foreign-language press in each group that was Communist controlled, though there would be serious limitations in the use of these figures as a measure of Communist influence. There are, first of all, technical problems in getting accurate figures. Ayer's *Directory of Newspapers and*

Periodicals gives for the foreign-language press a variety of sources for its figures: some newspapers have Audit Bureau of Circulation figures, some have Post Office estimates, some publishers' sworn statements, some only publishers' estimates. There is no tendency for non-Communist newspapers to give statements of higher reliability than Communist newspapers, if reliability is measured by the source and character of the estimate (sworn or unsworn, publisher or Post Office). Only for some non-Communist Yiddish newspapers are there any A.B.C. figures at all. And there is no way of knowing, without the most elaborate investigation, whether Communist newspapers exaggerated their circulation, and non-Communist did not, though this was so in one case (for the Yiddish newspaper).[86] Since the source and character of the estimates were similar, I accept them all for the purpose of constructing a simple measure of influence.

A more serious problem is raised by the role of newspapers published weekly, or more often, whose influence might be almost as great or as great as that of a daily newspaper. Properly to take into account the role of the weeklies would involve complicated judgments as to when a weekly is limited (literary, for women, and so forth) and when it serves as a regular newspaper. But in any case, in the larger ethnic communities, where a number of dailies circulate, dailies have a position quite distinct from any periodical that appears less often—and this is the case with every one of the communities dealt with here except the Croat.

Another important question is whether the circulation of a newspaper really represents Communist influence. People read newspapers for various reasons, and to get political interpretations is only one of them. Yet, when a number of newspapers circulate in the same immigrant community, to read the Communist newspaper regularly does tend to indicate a choice of political position. Reading the Communist newspaper probably tends to reinforce the political tendencies that have led to this choice. Moreover, the Communist language press was carefully supervised, and its errors corrected, sometimes by changes in staff.

But the fact must be borne in mind, too, that if the choice of newspapers is limited, as was the case in the Ukrainian group, and even more so in the Croatian group, many people may read the Communist newspaper even if they do not agree with it. For some reason, they may find the others even worse. Then, too, some of the newspapers preceded the split that produced the Communist Party, and some of their old readers may have continued to read them out of habit.

Nevertheless, the presence of a Communist daily does indicate influence in an immigrant community. Its influence is in part independent of its circulation, for it takes a considerable effort to support a daily newspaper. It requires a sizable staff —editorial, business, clerical, and skilled workers; it involves the ownership of presses; and if it runs at a deficit—as was generally the case—it involves fund-raising appeals and the organization required to carry out the raising of money. The need to raise money can be a source of organizational strength, as the Communists realized. Generally, the newspaper in the immigrant community became the center of the Communist work in that community. The editor and staff members were leaders in Communist work in that group, and the newspaper often had on its staff or attached to it organizers for work in that group (as, for example, in the cases of Silver and Lautner, mentioned above). For all these reasons, the presence of a daily newspaper may be taken as a sign of strength and, with greater caution, its circulation, compared with the circulation of competing newspapers, may be taken as a rough indication of Communist strength in the community. The following table gives the proportion of the daily newspaper circulation that was Communist in the eight foreign-language groups in which Communist newspapers were published in 1930 and 1935.

TABLE II · DAILY NEWSPAPER CIRCULATION IN FOREIGN-LANGUAGE GROUPS

	Number of dailies *		Circulation of all dailies (thousands)		Circulation of Communist dailies (percentage of total)	
	1930	1935	1930	1935	1930	1935
Croatian	2	1	30	14	53	†
Finnish	7	6	53	47	53	43
Hungarian	4	3	104	82	30	15
Jewish (Yiddish)	9	7	549.5	369	12**	13**
Lithuanian	4	4	100	92	48	33
Russian	3	4	65	70	35	31
Slovak	5	4	88.5	70	28	34
Ukrainian	2	2	32	28	47	47

* The Communist dailies were one in each group except for the Finnish, which had three in 1930, two in 1935, and the Lithuanian, which had two in each year.
† There was no Croatian Communist daily published this year; the Communist newspaper was at this time a weekly.
** These figures should probably be divided by three to make them accurate. See note 86 for this chapter.
Source: Ayer's *Directory of Newspapers and Periodicals,* 1930 and 1935.

As this table suggests, in some immigrant communities Communist influence was strong. In all these groups, there were also powerful opponents of the Communists, generally based on the immigrant elements that were attached to the church, or free-thinking elements that remained Socialist. Thus, the Finnish group also maintained a powerful Socialist and an I.W.W. daily. In the other groups, church influences were stronger.

But along with the degree of Communist influence in a group, the size of the group itself must be considered if any estimate of the importance of the group to the Communist Party is to be made. In the Latvian group, Communist influence was dominant,[87] but there were so few Latvians in the country that they could provide little in the way of membership or money to the Communist Party. In this context, the Jewish group presents a contrast. Despite the fact that Communist influence in it, as measured by newspaper circulation, was much smaller than among other ethnic groups, the Jewish group was the most important to the Communist Party, because it was by far the largest in which there was a Communist base of influence. In Table III are listed the major ethnic groups in the country, by mother tongue, in 1920, in order of size. Among the first three groups—German, Italian, and Polish—Communist influence was never great. The fourth in size is the Yiddish-speaking group. In the next four groups—the Swedish, French, Norwegian, and Spanish (at this date, mostly Mexican)—Communist influence was nonexistent or small. But in the ninth group—the Russian—the Communists were strong enough to maintain a daily newspaper. The Russian mother-tongue group in 1920 was not much larger than a third of the Yiddish mother-tongue group, however. And some of the Russian and the Hungarian mother-tongue group were assimilated Russian-speaking Jews and Hungarian-speaking Jews.

What explains the pattern of Communist strength among ethnic groups? Can it be said that the groups from Russia or the Russian borderlands tended to have a strong Communist

TABLE III · FOREIGN-LANGUAGE GROUPS, WHITE, IN THE UNITED STATES IN 1920

Mother tongue	(1) Foreign-born plus native of foreign or mixed parentage (thousands)	(2) Foreign-born alone (thousands)	(3) Percentage that foreign-born form of total group— column 2 over column 1
German	8,164	2,267	28
Italian	3,366	1,625	43
Polish	2,437	1,077	44
Yiddish	2,044	1,092	53
Swedish	1,485	643	32
French	1,290	467	36
Norwegian	1,021	362	32
Spanish	851	556	65
Russian	732	392	53
Czech	623	234	37
Slovak	620	275	44
Danish	467	190	41
Magyar	474	268	56
Dutch	370	137	37
Lithuanian and Lettish *	337	182	54
Finnish and Esthonian †	265	134	50
Greek	222	129	58
Portuguese	216	106	49
Slovenian	209	103	49
Croatian **	144	85	43
Syrian Arabic	104	58	56
Ruthenian	95	56	59
Rumanian	92	62	67
Flemish	88	46	52
Serbian ‡	57	40	70
Armenian	53	38	72
Bulgarian	14	13	93
Of mixed mother tongue	791	———	———

* The two groups are not divided in this census. The *Fifteenth Census of the United States* (1930), Vol. II, *Population*, Chapter VII, p. 347, does divide

element? This seems, in general, to be the case, with one important exception, and that is the Polish group. The Catholic church limited the appeal of Communism there. Yet the Catholic church was scarcely less powerful among Slovak and Croatian immigrants. And among Croatians and Slovaks, too, though in smaller measure than among Poles, the church was a national church.

The table of mother-tongue groups also includes a measure of assimilation and length of time in this country—the proportion of each group that is foreign-born. Perhaps time of immigration as such is related to attachment to Communism. But the newer groups were also the groups from Eastern Europe. These East European peoples, many of whom spoke languages close to Russian, many of whom were concentrated in heavy industry and worked under difficult conditions, responded to the Russian revolution and the appeal of Communism, and this response was most limited where a counterinfluence, such as a nationalistic Catholicism, was strong.

The evidence does not suggest more than that. It would not be possible to say that groups responded in the degree to which they suffered exploitation and unpleasant work. Certainly Poles and Italians had jobs that were not superior to those of the

---

these two groups, but only for foreign-born. There were 165,000 Lithuanian foreign-born to 8,000 Lettish. Something like this ratio probably obtained between the two groups in 1920.

† Again, the *Fifteenth Census* suggests the ratio that obtained between these two groups in 1920. For the foreign-born alone, there were in 1930, 125,000 Finns, 3,000 Esthonians.

** I have combined, to make this group, the categories in the census "Croatian" (141,000) and "Dalmatian" (3,000).

‡ I have combined, to make this group, the categories in the census "Serbian" (52,000) and "Montenegrin" (5,000).

Source: *Fourteenth Census of the United States* (1920), Vol. II, *Population*, Chapter 10, "Mother Tongue of the Foreign White Stock," p. 973.

Slovaks and the Croatians, while, by the 1920's, Jewish workers had somewhat better conditions of work.

Social causation is complex. Certain large general causes can be found that help explain the pattern of Communist influence. It is significant that no group from the older immigration supplied any permanent Communist base, and it might be concluded that the process of acculturation and assimilation among Germans, Irish, and Scandinavians had gone so far and working conditions were already so far improved (as compared with those of newcomers) that Communism had little appeal for them. But it is also true and perhaps more significant that a large part of these groups came to America before the rise of Socialism in their home countries. It is also significant that where Catholicism retained the strongest hold, and this was the case where it was closely identified with national aspirations, Communism was restricted, even in a new immigrant group.

But, as was suggested in Chapter I on the question why certain foreign-language groups in the Socialist Party supported the Left Wing and eventually the Communists, details of inner organizational history are also of great importance, particularly in relatively small groups. In each of these groups, there were battles over the control of newspapers and organizations. Undoubtedly, success in these battles was in part determined by organizational astuteness. Once such an organizational base was won for the Communists, it became subject to the processes whereby the Communist Party tried to turn its membership into Bolsheviks. Initially, there was probably little difference—if any—between Left-Wingers and Right-Wingers in each of these groups. It would be hard to prove, for example, that the workers in the Finnish and Jewish groups that went to the Left were generally more exploited and less petty bourgeois than the workers who stayed Socialist. Such a theory must be accepted on faith, as the Communists do; there is no evidence that anything like this happened. But once a Left-Wing group was established, it underwent a development which made it quite different from the group it had left behind. With Bolshevization, many of the new Communists were forced into units in which they worked with people outside their own ethnic group. Bolshevik tactics and language soon forged organizations and newspapers quite different from those of their former comrades. With the end of the factional fight in 1929, the processes by which Communists were "steeled" and "hardened" operated with ever greater effectiveness: attendance at schools; participation in mass demonstrations; handing out leaflets and selling the *Daily Worker* and the foreign-language newspapers and Communist literature; the vilification of fellow workers and fellow ethnic-group members as "social fascists" and "agents of imperialism"; duties in organizing workers, organizing the unemployed, in fighting "fascist" and "social fascist" influences in ethnic organizations. Every such action, if one survived it (and many did not and abandoned the party), made one a better Communist. By 1930, the processes whereby Communists are made had been routinized—and if one subjected oneself to them, or allowed oneself to be subjected to them, they were enormously powerful in creating men of a "new type" for the party of a "new type."

Workers from immigrant groups who found themselves in the Communist orbit, in part because they were in ethnic groups with a tradition of Socialist and working-class organization, in part because of the accidents of organizational history, were turned into these men of a new type and played an important role in the expansion of Communism, as it successfully reached social elements quite different from themselves in the 1930's.

THREE · NATIVE WORKERS AND TRADE-UNION INFLUENCE AND THE PARTY

T he party of the twenties presents relatively few problems to the social analyst. It remained small all through the decade. Its membership was consistently drawn from working-class elements of certain recent immigrant groups. The reasons for its small size and social composition may be found in its revolutionary policies, and, in particular, in its lack of understanding of the United States, in the prevailing economic prosperity from which all radical groups suffered, and in its close relationship to and undisguised subservience to the Comintern leaders in Moscow.[1]

The thirties are a very different story. First of all, the party grew rapidly (see Table IV). It doubled in the first three years of the Depression; it doubled again in the first two years of the New Deal; it almost doubled again in the following two years. And then for twelve years, from 1938 to 1950, the party was able to muster a membership of at least 50,000. Its power to recruit rose even more rapidly: 11,000 were brought into the party in 1931, 19,000 in 1932, 17,000 in 1933. And by the late thirties it could recruit 30,000 in a single year. (It lost almost as many—but that is another story.) ²

The composition of the party membership in the thirties and forties was much more varied than in the twenties. Three elements of this membership will be explored in this and succeeding chapters. The first element is the native American membership, which the party needed to give it influence and leadership among workers in factories and in the trade-union movement. The second is the middle-class membership, which from the middle of the thirties became quite large, and remained large throughout the forties. The third is the Negro element. These three categories correspond to certain problems of the party as the party saw them, and observations can thus be organized around them. This chapter will deal with the first.

The party wished to gain influence over large groups of workers and over trade unions. It spoke, therefore, of the need for "American-born workers" and "native American cadres," for the party thought that the members that could give it influence over industrial workers and their institutions should be native-born. Despite the foreign composition of the American working class, its leaders have always been the native-born or the English-speaking immigrants or the most Americanized of the foreign-language-speaking immigrants.

What would gain the party such influence? A worker in the shop, respected by his fellow workers, able to move them on one or another point, was one such means of influence. A shop nucleus, collecting a few such workers so they could co-ordinate their activities for the party, heightened this influence. A trade-union headquarters, local or national, controlled or influenced by the party formed another major level of influence.

Where did the party stand in terms of this kind of influence

TABLE IV · COMMUNIST PARTY MEMBERSHIP,
1930—1955 [3]

Date		Membership	Source
March—April 1930		7,500	Report to Communist International, 1935
	1931	8-9,000	Report to Communist International, 1935
	1932	12-14,000	Report to Communist International, 1935
	1933	16-19,000	Report to Communist International, 1935
February	1933	20,593	Report to Communist International, 1935
July	1933	15,000	Report to Central Committee, May 1935
	1934	24,500	Report to Communist International, 1935
May	1935	31,000	Report to Central Committee, May 1935
		26,815 (*registered*)	
October	1936	42,000	Public estimate by high party official, October 1936
January	1937	37,000 (*registered*)	Report to Central Committee, February 1938
January	1938	55,000 (*registered*)	Report to Central Committee, February 1938
April	1942	50,000	Report to National Committee, April 1942
		44,000 (*registered*)	
January	1945	65,000	Calculated from report to National Committee, November 1945
January	1946	52,500	Calculated from report by high party official, January 1947

TABLE IV · Continued

Date		Membership	Source
End of	1948	55-60,000	Estimate by John Lautner
	1949	54,174	F.B.I. estimate
January	1950	50-55,000	Estimate by John Lautner
	1950	43,217	F.B.I. estimate
End of	1951	31,608	F.B.I. estimate
	1955	22,663	F.B.I. estimate

3 Notes and sources can be found as note 3 on page 206.

in the early thirties? It had large numbers of workers in the shops and factories—but, as was seen in the last chapter, they were overwhelmingly foreign-born, many did not speak English, they were afraid to expose themselves by approaching fellow workers, and even afraid to expose their organizations by permitting others into them. Just as the American working class was fragmented by its varied ethnic origins, so, too, was the Communist Party.

There was only one area in which this ethnic affiliation of the individual worker was not a hindrance to effective party influence among fellow workers, as it certainly was in the coal mines, the steel mills, the auto plants. This was in those industries where almost all the workers came from the same ethnic group, where the workers' institutions were part of, rather than separate from, the ethnic culture, were even the employers were part of the same ethnic world. This was the case in the clothing industries, in which the workers were predominantly Jewish, in which the unions were Jewish—indeed, a good part of whose business was still conducted in Yiddish—in which even the employers were Jewish and could be influenced by public opinion in the larger Jewish community. Social life, work life, and union life were carried on in the same language and the same community. Here the situation of the Communist Party in a homogeneous nation was reproduced. Here the ethnic identification of the workers did not reduce their capacity to organize and fight as workers.

In the case of a Polish worker in the coal mines (and there were a good number who were close to the Communist Party), his identification as a Pole served as a barrier to other workers in the mine, it reduced his capacity to exert his full power in the English-speaking union, run by older ethnic elements (English, Scottish, Welsh, Irish), and of course it served to limit his ability to deal with foremen and employers. There were enough Jewish workers sufficiently concentrated in certain industries to form a Jewish labor movement in this country (this is the way the Jewish unions spoke of their unions and related institutions), but there was no Polish or Hungarian or Croatian or Slovak labor movement. It consequently became necessary for the workers in the Communist Party, if they were to have the impact on fellow workers that the party hoped for, to overcome the limitations imposed by working within, and feeling primarily identified with, an ethnic group. They were called upon to act primarily as workers, capable of making contact with fellow workers, of leading them, of forming unions for them.

There was, of course, a small group of native origin in the Communist Party throughout the twenties. The top leadership of the party in particular was generally native-born, or quite Americanized. This was so of Foster, Browder, Cannon, Gitlow, Lovestone, and many others. The English-speaking Section of the party grew more rapidly during the twenties. Yet Earl Browder asserted in 1935, when the situation in this respect had so improved that one could speak quite freely about the past, that in 1930 "there were less than 10 per cent native workers in the Party." [4]

Where did the few native-born members of the party come from? For the most part, they had been inherited from other radical groups, in the confused period while the party was being formed in the early twenties, and they were also recruited in small number from these groups during the twenties. One source for native-born members of the party during the twenties was the Industrial Workers of the World. Originally conceived of by the Comintern as a possible founding member organization for a Communist Party, the I.W.W. had decided not to affiliate with the Third International. The Communists nevertheless saw in the I.W.W. an important source of native working-class elements and continued to work on individual members of the I.W.W., and within the organization, in an attempt to get control of it. A historian of the I.W.W. estimated in 1932 that "Possibly the I.W.W. have lost as many as 2000 members to the Communists; possibly 10 to 20 per cent of the Communist party is now composed of former I.W.W.'s or former active supporters." He lists as former members of the I.W.W. who had gone over to the Communists and held important positions in the party the acting editor of the *Daily Worker,* a member of its editorial staff, the national secretary and the national organizer of the Marine Workers Industrial Union, and a leader in Communist union work in the Northwest.[5] During the twenties, a few native-born intellectuals also found their way into the party.[6]

The party's primary effort was continually to get native workers. "We cannot overestimate the importance of drawing larger numbers of American-born workers from the basic industries and developing from them leading cadres of the Party." [7] This was the perpetual theme of the early thirties. But meanwhile the great mass of the party was to be transformed into suitable agents.

Throughout its life, the party was engaged in alchemy—a human alchemy based on the proposition that a man could be stripped of his native social characteristics and changed into an agent who could then take on the social properties required for the tasks the party felt were most pressing. Elements that the party possessed in superfluity were to be transformed into elements that were scarce.

For this reason, the party was engaged in a continual self-survey of its social resources, of the social characteristics of the membership, of, as it was put, the "social composition." Such surveys permitted the party, first, to see if it was making the proper impact on the groups it most wished to influence; second, to see if it had enough cadres of different types for its tasks, on the simple and reasonable assumption that members could do their best work among those who were socially most like them; and third, to lay the groundwork for recruitment and training for the future.

So in the convention reports and in directions to members, the membership was divided into relevant categories: employed or unemployed, foreign-born or native-born, industrial or non-industrial, heavy or light industry, white or Negro, man or woman, trade-union member or not. It was better to have members who were employed, native-born, Negro, women, young, trade-union members, and in heavy industry. The reasons the party favored these categories may be found in the Leninist theory of the party and the revolution as developed by the Comintern leaders in the twenties. Some of these points of emphasis are obvious: the native-born because this was America; the youth because they were presumably more vigorous, and representative of the future; the employed because they could more easily get in touch with other workers; workers in heavy industry because that is the most crucial area. (There was here an interesting cultural lag. Heavy industry might be most important if one was interested in revolution and in paralyzing the economy. But if one was most interested in influencing opinion—and increasingly after 1934 this was the party's major emphasis—then the views of workers in heavy industry are possibly the least significant. Nevertheless, the party always maintained this emphasis.[8]) The emphasis on getting larger numbers of women members, which is constant throughout the history of the Communist Party, is interesting, and one is at a loss to understand it. In part, the small proportion of women members suggested that the numbers of party workers could be economically increased by the recruiting of sympathetic wives. In part, this may also be a heritage from Lenin himself, who was assisted by a group of competent women revolutionaries.

There were limits as to what could be done in transmuting the more common elements into the less common. Men could not be changed into women, the old into the young, whites into Negroes.[9] But workers in light industry could be sent into heavy industry, the foreign-born could be trained to work among the heterogeneous American working class, and (somewhat later) white-collar workers could be directed into factories.

Every party member (just as every human being) could make use of a number of social roles. Any individual might be simultaneously a steelworker, a trade-union member, of some given national origin, young, a veteran. The role he played in party work was often determined by the role in which he came into the party. Thus, if he came into the party through his connection with an ethnic group, it became difficult to get him to use his other social roles for party purposes. When the party called upon its members that each "turn his face to the factory," what it meant was that those who already worked in factories should see that the work among other workers in that factory was relevant party work.

The party alchemy consequently had two tasks: to make people take up new roles, and to have them recognize the significance for party work of roles they had not brought into play for this purpose. At this time, Slovaks were to see themselves as steelworkers, Finns as farmers. In later years, when the party seemed to have enough people in many unions, and began again to emphasize work in the ethnic communities, particularly with the second generation, the demand was reversed—now the steelworker was to become a Slovak, a union organizer a Croat.[10]

The principle remained the same throughout the history of the party: its specific application varied with the party's tasks and the composition of its membership. At this time, in the early thirties, there was a steady barrage in all the party organs to get the foreign-language members to conceive of their role as workers, related to the central task of the party. One of the many documents emphasizing this problem deals with the situation in Youngstown, Ohio, in 1934. It said in part:

One instance: The Section is in a chaotic situation because of the political and organizational bankruptcy of the previous Section leadership recently removed. Everything is upside-down, and great efforts are made to put things in order. The units are faced with urgent tasks. In unit No. — a South Slav language comrade proposes the postponement of the unit meeting, because the language comrades are engaged in rehearsing a play, and there is little time left to make the acting successful.

Another instance: a language comrade, on the evening of his local union meeting, goes to the headquarters of his "language society," to warm his feet. Since he is the chairman of the local, he was asked as to the reason for his not going to the local meeting.

"Hell, it is too cold, there is hardly gonna be anybody there, anyhow," he answered with a feeling of justification.

In the city of F—— non-party workers went to a comrade asking for advice because the workers were in a fighting mood in that particular steel mill and wanted to fight for wage increases. The comrade advises them to form committees, etc. The workers hand in a signed petition for a 20 percent increase in wages and they got it. Yet our comrade "forgot" to bring these workers into the S.M.W.I.U. [the Steel and Metal Workers Industrial Union, the Communist union then in the industry], they are busy with "language work" and rehearsing a play, "Struggle on the Barricades." [11]

Sometimes the party attack was directed not at the foreign-language members for not turning their face to the factory, but to the organizers who did not realize how many party members or potential party members lay hidden in the factories. "There are cases where a street unit that has concentrated for months on a given factory without any results discusses questions in a club while in the next room a language organization is holding a meeting in which workers from this particular factory are participating." [12] And even when these reluctant factory workers were flushed out by the persistent organizer, he might meet resistance. In one factory, where four party members were discovered, it was reported: "[Three of them] did not want a shop unit. They wanted to go back to their street units and continue functioning in their mass organizations—singing and language societies. The fourth . . . said he had no time because he was working on a language paper." [13]

This problem continued to loom large during the first few years of the Depression. But then the situation changed radically. First, the Depression made many desperate people susceptible to the party's appeals; then, the slogans of the Popular Front broadened even further the appeal of the party. In July 1933, the party was still 70 per cent foreign-born.[14] By May 1935, this proportion had dropped to 61 per cent. In October 1936, it was announced that for the first time the majority of the members were native-born. This was an important watershed in the history of the party. Even in the New York District, where the proportion of the foreign-born was greater, the native-born element rose rapidly—from 22 per cent in 1934, to 29.5 per cent in 1935, to an absolute majority in September 1938.[15]

But while the elements recruited during the early thirties were in the majority native-born, and while they were unquestionably of the working class, they were in some other respects unsatisfactory. The reason the party wanted native-born workers, as was indicated earlier, was in order to reach the workers in the factories, to "root the party in the factories." And the overwhelming majority of the recruits of the early thirties were unemployed. They were not in the factories.

The first great success of the party after the onset of the Depression was the unemployed demonstration of March 6, 1930, in which, according to party sources, more than a million workers participated in many cities.[16] Throughout the thirties, the Communists showed great skill and ability in organizing among the unemployed. Thus, in the first successful recruiting drive of the Depression, and the greatest in the party's history until then, 6,000 members were brought into the party. A high party official wrote: "During the drive the main weakness was recruiting largely from demonstrations of unemployed and mass meetings with absolutely insufficient recruiting from factories and trade unions." [17] Again in 1932 it was said that most of the new members were unemployed, "whom we have won over chiefly through unemployed mass work." [18] In 1933, again of the new members, it was said that "90 percent . . . are unemployed." [19] In the autumn of 1933, 60 per cent of the entire membership was unemployed.[20] In May 1935, 53 per cent of the party was unemployed and an even higher percentage—66 per cent—of a large group of recent recruits, indicating the party's continuing skill in reaching and organizing the unemployed.[21] In October 1936, almost half the party was still unemployed.[22]

Aside from limiting the possible impact of the party on the factories, the high percentage of unemployed membership probably contributed to another problem that plagued the party—the high fluctuation, or turnover of membership.

The great recruiting drive of 1930, in which 6,000 members were brought into the party, has already been referred to. But during 1930, the actual membership rose only about 1,000. In the following year, 12,000 new members entered the party, and the figures show an increase of only 4,000 or 5,000. In 1932, almost 19,000 new members were recruited into the party, but the increase was again only 4,000 or 5,000. In 1933, more than 17,000 members entered the party, and, again, the increase was only about 5,000.[23] In October 1934, it was reported that 17,000 new members had been recruited thus far that year, but the average number of dues payments was below that at the first of the year.[24] It cannot be assumed that it was the new members who moved in and out while the old ones remained stable. In April 1932, of 12,000 members, only 3,000 had been in the party before 1930, when it had about 7,500 members.[25] For the entire period from 1930 to 1934, 60,000 filled out application cards and paid initiation fees, and the increase in the party during this period was only about 16,000.[26]

The interpretation was as clear to the leaders of the Communist Party as it might be to a contemporary sociologist.[27] The unemployed, the uprooted, without connection to work places and working comrades, who joined out of despair and were weak in ideology, did not make the steadiest members,

and fluctuation would only be overcome when the party recruited more heavily from the employed. (But when, in the
late thirties, the party did begin to recruit predominantly from
the employed, the fluctuation was not reduced by much. There
were apparently other factors involved in the membership turnover.) [28]

In any case, the new members pouring into the Communist
Party, and the native-born and young among them, often had
little contact with heavy industry and factories, transportation
and mines. They had to undertake their work from the outside,
which aroused the suspicion of the workers, brought down the
violence of police and employers, and which, despite the opportunities for heroism it provided, was singularly ineffective in
penetrating the working class.[29] The typical pattern of outside
work was to get party members to "concentrate" on a factory,
which meant that they would hand out leaflets, try to get into
conversation with workers, and try to get them to come to meetings where a unit of the Communist union working in that industry might be organized, or a Communist nucleus organized
directly. (It was often left vague just what was being organized.)
If a strike broke out, the number of party members and organizers concentrating on the factory would suddenly increase.
In those days before mass union organization and bureaucrati-
zation, it was often possible for the Communists, totally unre-
lated to the workers on strike, to take over the leadership of
the strike, or at least play some role in it. In this way it was
hoped the party would get members for its union and itself.

One description of how this process operated is an account
of what happened during the Auto-Lite strike in Toledo in 1934.

The Party's first task . . . even though it had no organizational
contacts . . . not to speak of groups . . . with the strikers was
to give a line. . . . It brought down 100-200 workers from time

to time in the picket line and tried to fraternize with the union pickets. It issued many leaflets, held meetings, etc. . . . Only in the last days of the strike were there the beginnings of a rank-and-file group which has now grown to over 20. [Where a non-Communist union existed, as in this case, the Communists would commonly resort to the organization of a "rank-and-file" group.] Our being outside the union made it easier for fakers to refer demagogically to us as "outsiders." [30]

The conduct of outside work, it is clear, raised great difficulties, and it was, on the whole, without success until 1934.

It was better, obviously, to find a worker or workers who could do the party's work inside the factory. It was a victory to recruit even one insider. There always seemed to be far more people available outside a factory than inside one, and there was more joy in party headquarters over one worker really working in a shop than ten members not so strategically placed. And so such passages as the following are common in the party literature of the period: "We knew we had to have several developed comrades from the docks themselves to lead the rank and file work . . . what we did was to first concentrate on the four most likely contacts. Only one of them proved unsuitable for the Party . . . we have only eleven members of the outside unit [that is, the party unit assigned to "concentrate" there] who can appear on the docks. . . ." (The source does not explain why; perhaps their middle-class appearance or ethnic limitations raised too great obstacles.) [31]

Another favored approach was "colonization"—that is, placing a party member on the inside to work in a factory. The colonizers were drawn from the areas where there were many members, and from among the social elements of which the party had large numbers. Thus, one proposal was made that the unemployed in the big cities be sent to the small industrial towns.[32] Had the party had any large number of middle-class elements at this time, they would certainly have been urged or directed to go into the factories. As it was, the party had to depend on its membership in the light industries. "We have hundreds of steel workers in our union . . ." Browder said in 1933. "Are steel workers so incapable that we have to draw food workers and needle workers from New York to build the steel union?" [33] Indeed, they had to.

Under these circumstances, the onslaughts of outside and inside men, colonizers and concentrators, were not very effective.[34]

Somewhat different problems from that presented by a group of workers in a shop were presented by trade unions. While members in the shop meant members and, possibly, power in trade unions, this was not always the case. It depended on whether the trade union was so organized as to permit the sentiment of workers, themselves Communists or under the influence of Communists, to make itself felt. Alternatively, influence in or control over a trade union did not necessarily mean influence over the workers: the union might be small and unimportant, a simple headquarters organization. It seemed to be the unfortunate situation of the Communists that where they were strong among the workers they faced insuperable difficulties in influencing the unions; and vice versa.

The party had always insisted that every member be a member of a trade union. Just which trade union was a matter that changed as higher party tactics changed.[35] During most of the twenties, the policy of the party was to work within established trade unions in the A.F. of L. ("boring from within"). The A.F. of L. unions were, however, remarkably efficient and ruthless in hunting out Communists and driving them from leadership and even membership in the unions. Relatively large groups

of Communists within the United Mine Workers were totally
ineffective in gaining any strong center of operations against
John L. Lewis's powerful machine.[36] The leaders of sizable
groups in the Carpenters Union were expelled.[37] Only in the
needle-trade unions, with their large Socialist and Jewish memberships, was there some partial success. Among the fur workers the Communists captured a powerful base from which they
were not to be dislodged until the breakup of the party in the
late fifties, and they came close to seizing control of the large
International Ladies' Garment Workers' Union.[38]

The period of boring from within was succeeded by the radical "third period," beginning in 1928, when the Trade Union
Unity League was formed and a variety of revolutionary unions
independent of the A.F. of L. were created. The major ones were
the Needle Trades Industrial Union, the National Miners Union, the Food Workers Industrial Union, and the Steel and Metal
Workers Industrial Union. In some areas (the needle trades)
there were enough Communists so that the withdrawal of cadres
to create a new union did not strip the old unions of Communists. Most of the affiliates of the T.U.U.L. were weak, with
small bodies of members (again often based on devoted foreign-
language members), and with varying numbers of organizers,
depending on higher party policies as to where to throw the
party's weight.

Because the Communists were so weak in the factories, they
were also weak in the unions, and for the same reason. In the
unions, too, they had the problem of working from the outside.
As Earl Browder put it: "The reason why our unions that we rebuild and rebuild year after year don't stay built is because we
are doing it always with outside cadres, importing the cadres." [39]

In July 1933, the party membership was presented with an Open Letter, at an Extraordinary Party Conference, and summoned to intensify its efforts to recruit native workers in the basic industries—steel, mining, auto, textile, transport. A truly extraordinary effort was made to realize the directives of the Open Letter. From the seriousness with which it was taken, it was clear it came from the Comintern, though by this time a certain delicacy had developed in the party in referring to the source of such documents. The Open Letter coincided with developments quite independent of it which were finally to make the party an important force in the American labor movement, and to gain for it a powerful base among American workers.

What was the cause of the change from the relative ineffectiveness of the period from 1930 to 1933 to the successes of 1934 to 1938? The Communists, with their emphasis on the centrally directed manipulation of events, their distrust of "spontaneity," naturally ascribed it to the impact of the Open Letter and the decisions taken at the Extraordinary Conference. But these decisions were, after all, not original and unique. "As far back as the beginning of 1931," a critical survey of the party's work said in the organ of the Comintern in late 1932, "the party made a decision to concentrate the entire work in several of the most important regions, districts and factories." [40] These were the same decisions that were later to be taken at the Extraordinary Conference, and no significant consequences followed them in 1931. The party's successes in reaching the working classes after 1933 were the result of quite different events: the coming of the New Deal and the upsurge in the American labor movement which accompanied it. In the wave of strikes that began in 1933, the few Communists who had been working in factories and mines and shops found themselves, if they were at all competent, carried like corks riding a flood to top positions in a host of new unions.

The Communists had led important strikes in the past, in the twenties and the early thirties, but their gains in membership among the workers from these strikes had been insignificant. "We must learn the big lessons of the Passaic strikes, the New Bedford strikes, Gastonia, of the big miners strikes of 1927, which gave us hardly any new members to the Party and very few nuclei in the shops," asserted party leader William Weinstone in 1931.[41] His lessons, of course, had to do with the interminable refrain—organization, organization, organization. But there were other lessons of greater importance to be drawn from the party's failures in the strikes of the twenties.

First, these strikes were all lost, or, at best, were only partial victories, and it is difficult to build up organization in a losing strike. Second, in part because these strikes were lost, in part because this was before Section 7A of the National Recovery Act and the Wagner Act, no permanent, strong unions emerged from these strikes. In the face of the opposition or indifference of state and federal governments, it was very difficult to spread labor organization in the twenties and early thirties. Consequently, there was no organizational structure within which the Communists could work, use their skills, and recruit members. Third, and perhaps most important, in all the strikes Weinstone mentioned, except the miners' strikes, the Communists were not "in the shops"; they had to work from the outside, and therefore, with the end of the strike, the organizers scattered, and there was no cadre left behind to organize the party.

In 1933, all this changed. In the thirties, a huge labor movement was created, largely by the spontaneous organization of local unions by workers. The workers in these years of union creation went out looking for organizers and unions—rather than, as is generally the case, organizers and unions looking for workers.⁴² In the trade-union explosion of the thirties, Communists succeeded in placing themselves at the head of sizable groups of workers and creating and controlling important organizations. Just before the Open Letter, had come the inauguration of Franklin D. Roosevelt, and then the N.R.A., interpreted by organized labor as the signal that a government favorable to it had taken power. There followed the upturn from the trough of the Depression, and a great wave of strikes and the creation of large numbers of new unions.

In this situation, the few Communist organizers suddenly became important. They were now sought out, because they, too, represented some union, even if it was only a name and an office. Small radical groups of all kinds were able to achieve a fantastic degree of influence in the labor movement. A few adherents of Lovestone guided the president of the United Automobile Workers. A handful of Trotskyists at the head of a powerful Teamsters Union in Minneapolis wielded a large influence in the labor movement of that city and laid the foundation for extensive teamster organization covering a number of states.⁴³ The Communists, the largest, best organized, and best financed of these radical groups by far, were certain to be important beneficiaries of the upsurge in labor organization.⁴⁴

The creation of the International Longshoremen's and Warehousemen's Union, the organization that, under Harry Bridges, has remained for more than twenty years the most important base of Communist strength on the Pacific Coast, illustrates the process by which a few Communists were able to create or capture important organizations, and finally achieve a strong, native, working-class cadre. Before the outbreak of the longshoremen's strike in 1934, there was, despite great efforts and much expenditure of money by the party, not a single Communist member on the docks. Sam Darcy, Communist leader in San Francisco, reported: "Unfortunately, our Marine Workers Union, after having as many as four and sometimes six full-time functionaries in San Francisco alone, had not a single worker on the docks." [45] However, even without workers on the docks, the nature of strike activities in those hectic times assumed the presence of many outside sympathizers. The Communists were active on the strike committee, in the city, elsewhere on the Pacific Coast, and as far away as national headquarters in New York, guiding, exhorting, denouncing, publishing.

These activities, according to Darcy, were more harmful than helpful. The tender shoots of Communist influence were continually threatened by the blasts of orthodoxy. The strike committee was Communist-led, but the dogmatism of those not working on the docks often came close to destroying this base of power. "The Marine Workers Industrial Union [the Communist union] called on the striking longshoremen to resist the strike breaking efforts of the [A.F. of L.] International Longshoremen's Association [which was the union nominally running the strike]. The writing of such a sentence almost cost us our unity with the men." And again: "There was constant pressure from some comrades, particularly comrades who had nothing to do with the strike and were away from the immediate situation, to issue leaflets calling these fakers [the A.F. of L. leaders] all sorts of names—none of which the workers believed or would believe." On one occasion, the Communist *Western Worker* was so anxious to discredit the I.L.A. that it reported as fact an unconfirmed rumor about the signing of a separate pact in one of the striking ports. The workers interpreted this rumor as an effort by the shipowners to demoralize the striking men. When they saw the story in the *Western Worker,* "they were so enraged that the close relation between the strikers and the *Western Worker* hung in the balance by a thread." [46]

All these and other hazards described by Darcy were successfully overcome. By the end of the strike, the Communists were no longer working from the outside. Halfway through the long strike Darcy wrote: "We have recruited to date, in San Francisco alone, about 25 longshoremen, and over 50 seamen; in San Pedro about 40 . . . and in the Northwest ports, many more." [47]

This was only the smallest part of the membership gain occasioned by a successful strike and the successful creation of a labor-union base. The publicity value of such a success among other workers, and among middle-class, professional, and intellectual sympathizers, was enormous. The strike lasted from March 23 to July 31. Browder reported that San Francisco membership, which had been 2,100 in May (and this must already have reflected the influence of the strike), rose to 3,000 by August. During the same period, in Pittsburgh, where there was no great struggle going on, the membership fell from 1,100 to 800.[48]

There was one more big strike before Bridges' union was successfully established, in 1936-37. During this three-month strike, 300 new members were recruited from among the striking workers, and 2,000 in all California.[49] With a few hundred members in a union of about 13,000, Communist influence was secure (100 members among 10,000 kept secure control of the Fur Workers Union).[50] And the gains were enormous. Through control of a union in the glamorous maritime industry, the party had living proof that its claim to represent the proletariat was no myth. Its influence in liberal middle-class circles was greatly increased by control of the union. Then there were union jobs, which meant that the party could recruit and control party members, using jobs as carrot and stick. Domination of the union permitted participation in local and national trade-union circles, which still further extended the influence of a relatively small group of Communists.

The West Coast longshoremen represent one of the great successes of the Communist Party in establishing a native working-class base, but there were others. A powerful union run by Communists was built among the East Coast sailors. An important part of the West Coast lumbermen and sawmill workers was organized in Communist-controlled unions. A powerful union run by Communists was organized among New York subway workers, a largely Irish working force. And in all these cases the same pattern can be traced—small groups of Communists were lifted to the leadership of mass unions by the great upheaval which transformed the American labor movement. In a trade union (as in any organization), enormous advantages are held by the first leadership group. Aside from these organizational advantages, the Communists were in fact founding fathers, with all the moral authority that gives a leader.

This was only one pattern by which Communists rose to leadership of unions. In some industries and unions they already had sizable groups of members: the needle trades, the food industry in New York (restaurant and cafeteria workers), the auto industry in Detroit, the steel mills, and the coal mines. In these industries, their success was variable, and depended on the organizational fighting skill of the opposition. It may be said as a general rule that the presence of a large group of Communist workers in a union produces in time (unless the Communists are completely victorious and expel the opposition) a knowledgeable and effective opposition. Twenty Communists in a union which had no experience with them might thus accomplish more than 200 in one which had experience in fighting Communists.

In the garment trades, the Communists controlled only the fur workers, and were reduced to ineffective oppositions in the other unions. Among the food workers, they had a powerful base in the New York locals.[51] In the United Automobile Workers, the Communists had a sizable membership. Jack Stachel, then organization secretary, estimated they had 1,500 members in the union in 1938, when it had about 400,000 members.[52] They had powerful non-Communist allies, leaders who had participated in the great sit-down strikes, as well as the constant attention and concern of the chief national leaders of the party. Yet they were defeated in their effort to control the union. For a time, they maintained control of important locals, and controlled the Ford local as late as the early 1950's.[53]

In one other industry in which they had a sizable membership, steel, the fate of the Communists was the most peculiar, and will serve to demonstrate the subtle relationship that existed between the Congress of Industrial Organizations and the Communists. The steelworkers were organized directly under the supervision of John L. Lewis, U.M.W. leaders conducted the drive, and U.M.W. members formed a large part of the organizing staff. This was the first time in American history that an organizing drive had used such a large staff and been conducted on such a massive scale. Under the circumstances, every competent organizer was welcomed, and a large number of Communists were among them. The Communists joined in the task of organizing the steelworkers with enthusiasm. One of their most skilled labor leaders, Bill Gebert (Boleslaw Gebert), was assigned the task of mobilizing Communist Party forces for the steel drive. Here the Communist strength among the foreign-language fraternal groups proved useful. Gebert organized big

conferences of these organizations to help launch the steel organizing drive. William Foster claims an important role for the
party in the drive, and with some justice.[54] And yet, despite the
Communist workers in the steel mills, despite the Communist
organizers who worked in the drive, the party gained no important sphere of influence in the union. A skillful anti-Communist administration, keeping close reins on local unions and
preventing the development of local autonomy, also prevented
the establishment of a Communist base in the Steel Workers
Organizing Committee.[55]

The C.I.O. employed Communist organizers and accepted
the affiliation of Communist unions. It also had a powerful Communist group in the national office. Its local federations (city
industrial councils) were often dominated by Communists, owing
to the large number of Communist unions—even though with
small membership—represented on these bodies. But if the
Communists controlled national C.I.O. unions, it was not because of national C.I.O. support. It was because of their luck
in being in on the ground floor when the unions were being
organized, or because they had a strong body of members in
the industry, or because of an ignorant or unskillful union administration.[56]

The large number of white-collar and professional unions
which the Communists organized do not quite fit into either of
the two patterns described—that in which a union was organized in an industry with few Communists (the I.L.W.U.),
and that in which the industry contained a good number of
Communists (the Auto Workers). The white-collar and professional unions contained a sizable number of Communists,
though the industries did not, for these unions organized only
a tiny fraction of their potential membership. Their problems
are special, and are discussed in the next chapter.

The upsurge of union organization, then, did create for the first time a large number of unions under Communist control. But, strangely enough, it did not solve the problem of rooting the party in the working classes. Indeed, in many respects the party was less of the working class in the late thirties than in the early thirties. For one thing, the professional and white-collar membership of the party rose even faster than the working-class membership. And second, the Communists were unsuccessful in transforming the unions they controlled into unions of Communist workers.

During the thirties, the party was transformed from a largely working-class organization to one that was one-half middle-class. In January 1932, the occupations of 6,500 members in five major districts were reported. A little more than 5 per cent of the membership fell into the category of "office" and "intellectual" workers. For May 1935, there is an analysis of the occupations of most of the membership; about 10 or 11 per cent appear to be middle-class members (taking the categories "office," "teachers," "artists," "sales clerks," and "storekeepers" as middle-class). In 1938, the breakdown of the occupations of a large group of new recruits (17,000) showed 22 per cent in middle-class categories. In 1941, no less than 44 per cent of the party was reported as professional and white collar.[57]

On the other hand, a look at the membership the party had in various industries (see Table V) shows that even in industries where the party had a powerful base, it did not have what might be called a mass membership; it came close to this only in marine and longshore groups. There, in view of the relatively small size of the industries involved, its membership seemed more than adequate for its organizational tasks. The table illustrates a number of other important points. Where the Communists failed to control the union in an industry, they at best

TABLE V · PARTY MEMBERSHIP IN SELECTED INDUS-
TRIES

	May—July 1928	May 1935	1939	April 1942
Total Party Membership	10,000	27,000	50,000(?)	50,000
Building Trades	986	2,423	———	2,100
Needle Trades	1,527	2,177	———	1,900
Food	400	1,373	———	1,200
Steel	———	700	2,000+	852
Metal	851	1,250	———	1,648
Mining	1,200	1,073	1,300	289
Auto	407	550	1,100	629
Marine	33	406	———	611
Warehouse & Longshore	———	———	———	805
Lumber	163	222	———	360

Sources for this table are those given in note 57 on page 215, and *The Communist*, April 1929, pp. 182-183.

managed to maintain their membership in the industry, and more
commonly suffered a decline. Where the Communists controlled
a union, their membership in the industry rose. The reasons for
this are that Communists were brought into unions they controlled from other industries, where they were perhaps check-
mated by an anti-Communist administration, and given union
jobs, or jobs in the shops from which they rose to union office.
Further, in the unions the party controlled, it was able, because
of its strategic position, to recruit union activists; many joined
because they saw no other way of achieving high position in
the union.[58] In 1938, an article in a Communist International
periodical, reporting on a successful recruiting drive of the party,
pointed out that "a surprisingly large number [of the new

members] are union officials. . . . A mere glance at the composition of the people that it is winning proves that beyond doubt . . . its work in the unions, especially in the Committee for Industrial Organization drives, has won to its ranks some of the most active union functionaries and rank and file workers." [59]

The important conclusion from this table is that even though the party had increased fivefold since the late twenties, there had been no such increase in the cadres in important industries. The party strength in the unions—except for maritime and longshoremen, and the white-collar unions—was not a mass-membership strength. It was based on organizational control. And it was largely by means of a battle between top organizational groups that it was thrown out of its powerful position in the labor movement when the C.I.O. administration turned against it in 1948.

With the rise in the proportion of white-collar and professional workers in the party came a rise in the proportion of the party concentrated in New York. New York made up only 22.5 per cent of the party in 1934, after the first increases in strength based largely on the recruitment of unemployed. This rose to 35 per cent in 1934, 47 per cent in 1938, and from then on, New York made up half of the party. A detailed F.B.I. breakdown by states for 1951 shows 51 per cent of the party in New York.[60] The New York party was much more heavily white-collar and professional, much more in light industry, than the party as a whole. In 1942, for example, the party's industrial composition had risen, as a result of the general shift into war work and the drafting of persons in nonessential occupations, to 47 per cent, and the basic-industrial composition had risen to 17 per cent (mining, steel, metal, auto, and transport). New

York's basic-industrial composition was only 7 per cent, and the "overwhelming" majority of the New York District Communists were in white-collar work and light industry.[61] The New York membership retained this characteristic. When the industrial composition of the party declined after the war, the New York party became even more middle-class. In March 1946, John Williamson reported that only 29 per cent of the New York party were industrial workers. California, then the second biggest district, had 38 per cent industrial workers. By contrast, "Michigan, which always has the highest industrial composition, has declined from 66 percent to 58 percent." [62]

Despite the party leaders' dismay at large numbers of middle-class members, it should not be concluded that New York and the middle-class membership formed the flabby part of the party, while the workers in heavy industry and in the unions formed the hard core, tried, dependable, preventing the white-collar and petty-bourgeois influences from softening the party's Leninist rigor. The reality was quite different. It was from New York that the cadres came; it was New York that was steady and dependable, while the trade-union leadership and industrial membership was often in danger of defection and softening. In certain unions—the International Longshoremen's and Warehousemen's Union, the International Union of Mine, Mill & Smelter Workers—the core of Communist trade-union and industrial strength approximated the Leninist image. But on the whole, the middle-class elements in the party were probably steadier and more dependable than the industrial part.

In Michigan, for example, with its consistently high industrial membership, turnover was also frightfully high. In January 1945, two-thirds of the membership in Detroit, John Williamson reported, had been in the party less than a year. The party there had as high a membership as ever. But "we suffer from the absence of an experienced cadre trained in long years of struggle. In New York City, where we have a corps of five or six thousand members of some years' standing in the Communist movement . . . the problem is not aggravated." [63] It was the heavy industrial areas that needed organizational strength from the outside. At the end of 1945, Williamson proposed sending in top cadremen coming out of the army to build up the party in six industrial areas: Youngstown, Gary, Flint, McKeesport, Toledo, and Kansas City.[64] In 1948, Henry Winston, who had succeeded the deported John Williamson as organization secretary, reported that efforts would be made to get white-collar and professional workers, veterans and students, to secure work in basic industry—a new emphasis on colonization, as in the early thirties.[65] Just who these new colonizers were may be discovered in a House Un-American Activities Committee report that was published six years later. At hearings in Flint, twenty-seven colonizers were discovered. Most of those the committee questioned had come from New York and had college educations. It was these petty-bourgeois elements which the party could deploy in the automobile plants of Flint.[66] Apparently, Communist leaders as well as farmers and small-town dwellers believe in the myth of the parasitic city in the face of all the evidence to the contrary.[67]

The analysis of membership statistics provides only a part of what is needed for the proper understanding of the basis of Communist trade-union strength. While some Communists were necessary to penetrate and capture a union, and some of these had to be workers in the industry, the relationship of these Communists to the organization was the final determinant of Communist power. A large number of Communists helped (as in the longshoremen's union), but in other circumstances (as in the Auto Workers) the Communists were balanced by equally large or larger numbers of committed adherents of other political tendencies, or ideological anti-Communists whose only commitment was to the union.

The organizational patterns were varied. In one situation, the New York Transport Workers Union, a union composed largely of Irish Catholics and run by an Irish Catholic was (or seemed to be) securely in Communist hands. But here the increase in membership that generally followed Communist control did not occur, even with the availability of union jobs and posts of union power. When Michael Quill, president of the union, decided to break with the Communists, there were too few in the New York Transport Workers Union to fight him to keep it in the party's hands.[68] In Joseph Curran's National Maritime Union, on the other hand, with its more mixed membership, the party had great membership strength. When Curran broke with the Communists, he had to fight a desperate struggle before he wrested control of the union from them.[69]

In the light of the various histories of many unions, large generalizations appear to be crude and clumsy, scarcely helpful in explaining any single outcome. To understand what happened in the Transport Workers Union, it may be enough to know that the great majority of the membership was Irish Catholic and immune to the party's appeals. It may be helpful to know that the West Coast longshoremen (Communist union) are a mixed and Americanized group, while the East Coast longshoremen (anti-Communist union) are broken up into encapsulated ethnic enclaves. Yet if it had been the West Coast longshoremen who were dominated by a violently anti-Communist union, and the East Coast longshoremen who were dominated by a Communist union, instead of the other way around, this variation in membership characteristics could be used to help explain that quite different outcome. As it was, when it came to the sailors, the two coasts changed places—the West Coast sailors were in an anti-Communist union, the East Coast sailors in a Communist-controlled union. And will any study of the characteristics of the membership help in understanding that phenomenon more than the fact that Harry Lundeberg, leader of the West Coast sailors, had learned to become suspicious of Communists because of his contact with the I.W.W.? [70] One of the most subtle of investigations of the relationship between the social characteristics of the membership of a union and its political structure is forced to conclude that the details of its history, the turning points affected by a hundred minor factors that may by now be quite unrecoverable, explain as much as the systematic analysis of its present membership.[71]

Conditions in an industry may help make workers more susceptible to radical appeals. For example, S. M. Lipset has argued that where the workers live in their own communities, are more cut off from contact with middle-class elements, and tend to be isolated for long periods of time, they will be more radical.[72] Thus miners, sailors, lumbermen may be expected to be radical. There would seem to be much truth in this general position. But what the specific radical outcome will be in any situation will vary greatly, depending on other circumstances. Thus, it is probably these isolating characteristics of coal miners that led them to obey, without qualms about national security, John L. Lewis's orders to strike during World War II. It is probably the removal of the New York longshoremen from middle-class influences that makes it easy for them to support a leadership that is denounced by every respectable institution in the land. Thus they are both "radical." But in this case what makes them "radical" also insulates them from Communist influence.

In the end, it would seem to be the organizational factors that predominate: the skill and training and luck of Communists and their opponents. Vernon H. Jensen has written in fascinating detail the history of the Mine, Mill and Smelter Workers Union, where Communist influence has remained paramount despite all the efforts of internal opposition, the national C.I.O., powerful raiding unions, and the U.S. Government. He has also written the history of the lumber workers. There came a time in the history of both the Mine, Mill and Smelter Workers and the International Woodworkers when Communist control hinged on a single organizational tactic. In both unions, the majority of the politically conscious membership was anti-Communist. In both cases, the Communists knew they would go down to defeat in union elections that placed Communists against anti-Communists. In both cases, they proposed to their opponents a "unity slate": that is, the membership or convention would be denied the opportunity to reject a fully Communist slate in favor of an anti-Communist slate, but would, instead, be presented by the union leadership with a single ticket, including some of the Communist leaders. In this way at least some positions of union power might be maintained for the party, and it could wait out the present storm for a better day. In the Mine, Mill and Smelter Workers, the opposition accepted this maneuver; in the International Woodworkers, they rejected it. The future fate of Communist control in both unions hinged as much on these moments as anything else that can be discovered. It would seem to be the case that a small margin of political sophistication saved the lumber workers from Communist control.[73]

The decline of Communist power in the trade unions was clearly related to the change in the international scene that led to the decline in power of the Communist Party in general. When Russia and the United States emerged as antagonists after World War II—and antagonists that touched each other directly or through their allies, along a 10,000-mile border—American Communism came under the attack of the U.S. Government, and Communists became something not very different from traitors.

In terms of industrial membership and organizational control, the party was probably as strong in 1948 and 1949, when the C.I.O. turned against it, as it had ever been before. As stated earlier, the industrial-worker membership of the party rose during the war, when many white-collar workers were drafted or became factory workers. At the end of the war, the proportion of industrial workers declined. Strong efforts were then made to raise the proportion of the members in industry and heavy industry, and according to the party's breakdown of its composition (Table VI), these efforts were successful. In September 1948, the party claimed a peak in industrial-worker membership higher than that attained during the war. The proportion of members in basic industry remained low.

Thus the party did not show any falling off in strength among workers during the postwar years. But in one essential respect this industrial membership was not of as high a quality as the rest of the membership, professional and white-collar. When the proportion of members in the industrial and basic industrial categories is compared with the proportion among new recruits, it can be noted that the party was much more successful in recruiting such elements than in retaining them. It seems to have been a general rule that when the party made the strongest efforts to get members, the members it got were the least satisfactory. Thus, just as when in the early twenties it recruited large numbers of English-speaking members but found it difficult to retain them, the same thing occurred in connection with the attempt to build up the industrial-worker strength of the party in the forties.

One does not have to look far to understand the reasons for

TABLE VI · INDUSTRIAL AND BASIC-INDUSTRIAL MEMBERSHIP OF PARTY, 1942—1948 (% of Total Membership)

	Jan. 1942	Jan. 1943	Jan. 1944	1946	Late 1946	Sept. 1948
Industrial membership in register of party members	47	43	46	39	43	51
Industrial membership among new recruits	——	62*	58†	57**	——	——
Basic-industrial membership in register of party members	17	23	27	19	22	18.5
Basic-industrial membership among new recruits	——	36*	38†	34**	——	——

* 15,000 members were recruited during the first few months of 1943, and form the base of these percentages.
† 20,000 members were recruited during the first few months of 1944, and form the base of these percentages.
** 15,000 members were recruited during the first six or seven months of 1946, and form the base of these percentages.
Sources: "Organization and Statistics, National Committee, April 5, 1942" (Browder Files); *Political Affairs*, June 1943, p. 540; June 1944, p. 521; September 1946, p. 814; January 1947, p. 69; September 1948, p. 839. During the entire period the membership of the party was between 50,000 and 60,000.

this. Members in the categories that the party did not favor entered the party because they wanted to, because they were committed, because they believed in the party; among such members efforts to recruit were relatively mild. Members in the categories the party favored—the English-speaking, the industrial workers, Negroes—were given every incentive to enter the party. They were pushed into party jobs, where these were available, they were flattered, they were urged to come in when their understanding and commitment were weak. Under the circumstances, they flowed out almost as fast as they entered; which is why the party in Detroit in 1946 consisted so largely of new elements, while the party in New York had a large and tested cadre.

The party therefore had to depend upon a wavering trade-union membership to resist the onslaughts of the C.I.O. and the government. In addition, the structure of party control in trade unions was rather different in 1948 from what it had been in 1938. In the late thirties and early forties, the party changed the nature of its control over the unions from control through fractions of party members to control through regularly elected union officials who were Communists or close friends of the Communists.[74] As former Communist agitators became important elected union officials, they also in many cases became annoyed at having to consult on policy with the fraction of Communist members in the union. It was more in keeping with their actual position and power to consult directly with the district leader, the trade-union secretary of the party, or the head of the party itself. The party seemed willing to accept the elimination of the fraction in those unions that were controlled by devoted party members or persons close to the party. But the party union leader was also a *union* leader, and if he wished to, he might be able to shift his base of power from the party and its members to the union and its staff. In a party-controlled union, the two were in large measure identical, but the same influence that might lead him to approve actions favoring union objectives rather than actions favoring party objectives (where the two conflicted) might influence the party members on the union staff in the same way.

Many evidences can be found of concern among the party leaders as to whether the union leaders would remain strong in their party faith, particularly when the party had to call upon the union leaders to do unpleasant things (as during the period of the Nazi-Soviet pact, and during the cold war after the end of World War II). Thus, Roy Hudson, then trade-union secretary, pointed out in October 1939: "Unless all Communists, especially those occupying leading posts in the trade union movement, constantly increase their knowledge of the basic party policies, they will soon be unable to provide the same high quality of leadership that they were able to give in the days of organized fraction work." [75] On the other hand, during the "soft" periods, the party seemed almost gentle in its willingness to let the Communist union official run his own show, as long as his basic loyalty was assured. John Williamson said in September 1942:

> Whereas yesterday, in many localities, shops and industries, the Communist Party was almost the exclusive medium of trade union activity [that is, for party members] . . . today all these functions are correctly handled by the trade unions themselves. Many workers, especially among the local trade union leadership, who are today more experienced but also more overloaded with union activity, while still agreeing generally with the Communist Party, nevertheless do not feel the same necessity for active party membership as they once did. . . . We cannot deny the existence of this problem or brush it aside. . . . *Today our political leadership must be of such a quality, depth and timeliness that it will be indispensable for every advanced and thinking American, especially every trade unionist and leader, to treasure membership in the Communist Party.*[76]

During the war, the Communist union leaders were treated with kid gloves by the party. Initially, their jobs had been gained through the power of the fraction and the party; now, established in the semipermanent tenure of trade-union leadership, they could draw on an independent base of power. The party seemed to be under pressure from the union leaders to disband the dual centers of power, and seemed, on the whole, anxious to do so. John Williamson wrote in 1943:

> All the fears by trade union leaders or other leaders of the war camp [this is a positive epithet at the time, of course] as to consequences of party growth must be dispelled by proving in life that

the Communist Party's growth . . . contributes to the strengthening of the organizations and the unity of the trade unions. . . . It . . . makes imperative the liquidation of all fractional methods of work in the trade unions, and methods of leadership in the trade unions whereby a District Organizer or any party leader becomes a broker or middleman between the trade union leaders who are party members and other . . . trade union leaders. . . . We must put an end to anything that might be interpreted as interference with the normal functioning of the trade unions, including those with Left and progressive forces in the leadership.[77]

In 1947-48, the party decided to encourage the creation of a third political party under Henry A. Wallace, and the trade-union leaders were required to toe a political line that they knew was anathema to the top C.I.O. leadership. Defections of union leaders began—Curran, of the National Maritime Union, then Quill, of the Transport Workers, and the allies of the Communists in the Auto Workers. Most of the Communist trade-union leaders, however, stood firm and were expelled by the C.I.O. The complex factors that permitted some to retain their unions, and in other cases led to the loss of the unions to non-Communist leaderships, or their reduction to mere shells, has been discussed. Whether a different organizational pattern— for example, the retention of the fractions in the unions—would have increased Communist strength (as some leaders believed) became a moot point.[78]

In any case, once an alternate power base existed for a Communist Party leader, it appeared that he, not the party, held the major reins of power. He could always go it alone, and could gain by his defection greater power in the labor movement, and the reputation of a patriot. In such a situation, it was chiefly one element that held a man to the party: the degree to which he had become a Communist, that is, his ideological commitment, which carried as a consequence a life lived in a party framework, with party people. Men who had done this—Harry Bridges appears to have been one—could not break with the party; perhaps it was as inconceivable for them to think of such a possibility as it would have been for William Z. Foster to.

In general, it would seem that the trade-union membership, weaker in ideological commitment, and with an alternative to the Communist Party available in the trade-union movement, was less dependable than the white-collar and professional membership. An interesting social psychological study compares a group of trade-union party members with one of intellectual party members. The groups are small (eighteen trade-union members, twenty-four intellectuals), and hardly random, but then, how is one to find a random sample of former Communists? The study found that when trade-union people joined the party, they made less of a break with their former lives, "making less of a social commitment, experiencing less of the 'party atmosphere' than non-trade union people." This is understandable. Trade-union work is prime activity for the Communist, and he will not be disturbed or required to do other things while he does it. The intellectual is generally taken out of his normal life and forced to work with the working class; the working-class and trade-union member remains in his life. The study notes that when the trade-union member breaks with the party, he characteristically retains his job, whereas the intellectual who leaves the party generally loses his, for the front group, for which he is likely to work, is entirely the creature of the party, while the trade union has an independent legitimate function. This means that it is easier for the trade-union man to leave the party.[79]

When the party decided, in 1950, under the attack of the government, that it must prepare to go underground, it ruthlessly reduced the party rolls to those who might be considered most dependable. This reduction was carried out by the cadres, the men who, regardless of origin, were Communists, and thought only as Communists, not as trade-union members, workers, Negroes, professionals, white-collar workers. It is interesting to see who went when they cut off the undependables. Henry Winston, the organization secretary, in one of those typical attempts to "correct" an excess by which the truth about what is going on in the party may be discovered, warned that there had been a radical reduction of industrial workers in this process:

> In one district there was a large club in a steel plant. Out of the total membership the conclusion was drawn that only 9 percent were eligible for registration, with a possibility of 4 or 5 percent more. The remaining 86 percent were to be dropped . . . in one area only 5 percent of the rubber workers were to be registered. . . . The lopping-off approach reduces our working class composition in general and our Negro workers in particular.[80]

In 1953, "Alex Parker" (the pseudonym of a high party official), giving the leading organizational report at a national conference of the party, asserted: "There has been a serious decline of industrial workers in the past several years. During the registration of 1950, which revealed serious liquidationist tendencies, our industrial losses were greatest." [81]

What, then, may be concluded from this investigation of the trade-union and industrial-worker strength of the party? The party was successful in its attempt to control a part of the American labor movement for a while, but it was less successful in drawing large numbers of effective party workers from the industrial working class. It eagerly welcomed them into the party, but since they entered out of curiosity, temporary resentment, or the desire for personal advantage, they left almost as rapidly.[82] It is true that part of these trade-union members—as is true of almost every group of members in the party—became members of the cadre. There are rich possibilities for ambiguity and irony in the fact that as they entered the cadre they lost the specific and concrete characteristics that had once made them workers—which, of course, was true of any member who was turned into a cadreman. But the cadreman does use his past symbolically, for whatever use he can make of the associations it may call up, sometimes referring to his Irish past, sometimes to his working-class history. However, the Communist Party never drew as many devoted members from the industrial working class as it wished.

FOUR · JEWS AND MIDDLE-CLASS GROUPS AND THE PARTY

T he Communist Party has always spoken of itself as the "vanguard of the proletariat," though it had enormous difficulties in realizing this extravagant slogan. But from the middle thirties to the early fifties, the period of its greatest size and its greatest influence, the party was rather more successful in becoming the "vanguard of the intellectual and professional workers." This middle-class cast to the American Communist Party differentiated it from almost every other Communist Party in the Western world. Another characteristic of the membership of the American Communist Party that differentiated it from almost every other Communist Party in the Western world was that a large proportion of its members were of Jewish origin.[1] (This is very different from saying that any large proportion of American Jews were Communists, for whereas the party membership only rose briefly above 50,000, there were in the thirties and forties 4,500,000 American Jews.) Neither of these peculiarities can be understood without the other. The party was so heavily middle class in large part because it was so heavily Jewish. But it is not easy to unravel the threads of explanation that connect these two phenomena.

To begin with, the major sources—the party and the government—rarely speak directly about the Jewish membership of the Communist Party.[2] From the party's point of view, to discuss straightforwardly the question of the Jewish membership would have been to raise doubts as to the party's success in reaching and representing the American working class;[3] from the point of view of the government agencies, there would have been enormous political repercussions in discussing such a question.[4]

And of course it was not in the interest of Jewish organizations themselves to publicly discuss such a matter. During the twenties, there were strong anti-Semitic tendencies in American life. During the thirties and forties, the Jews throughout the world were subjected to a murderous and irrational attack, one of whose major tenets was that they were "Communists" and subversive of all decent and respectable institutions.

The first problem in discussing the Jewish membership in the party, then, is the lack of published material, from both party and nonparty sources. The second is the important matter of the uses to which such material may be put by anti-Semites, who are not interested in understanding a problem, but in using the material that is a basis for understanding as a weapon of attack —in the same way one would be given pause in discussing the Negro proportion among criminals by the use to which such information might be put. Any responsible writer must ask himself whether this is a subject that may be discussed publicly. I believe that no detailed understanding of the impact of Communism on American life is possible without an analysis of the relationship between American Jews and the American Communist Party. As to whether such an analysis is required for any general, popular understanding of Communism, I think it is not. There were certain special reasons in the history of the relatively small Jewish Communist group that led it to play a disproportionate role in the American Communist Party and in a few other Communist parties (particularly the Canadian). In writing a general history of Communism, its relationship to Jews would be a relatively minor matter. But in the United States, this was not a minor matter, and does require analysis.

There is a third difficulty in discussing this problem. In what sense were the people called "Jews" in the party actually Jews? And who is to be discussed in considering the "Jewish element" in the party? There were the Yiddish-speaking—and among these, there were those committed to some Jewish interest (Yiddish or the survival of the Jewish people) and others who had no interest at all in any Jewish concern. There were the assimilated immigrants—and among them were many who had become assimilated to another culture before coming to this country, and who had a choice as to what to be, Jewish (and what kind), Russian, English. Leaders in work among Hungarians and Russians were often Jews. There were those who were born in this country, who did not speak Yiddish, who had no religious and national interests, whose whole life was the Communist Party, and whose first contact with any Jewish organization perhaps was when they joined it for infiltration under party orders. Were they "Jews"? And did their "Jewishness" have anything to do with their Communism?

Jewish members of the Communist Party included such different types as the children of Communists, some raised in what were, in effect, Communist communities; the children of other radicals; the children of the ordinary run of liberal-minded Jews. And there were those who were neither immigrants nor the children of immigrants, the wealthy sons of German-Jewish

families, intellectuals of non-Jewish backgrounds, liberal phil-
anthropists, and social workers.

As pointed out in Chapter II, the Jewish group was the largest
ethnic group from which the Communist Party drew sizable
membership elements. And the length of time over which Jews
emigrated to this country, the variety of their national and cultural backgrounds, the rapidity with which they moved from one
socio-occupational stratum to another created, perhaps, a greater
diversity among Jews than among other ethnic groups. Once the
diversity of the Jews who entered the Communist Party is realized, any simple interpretation of the relationship between Jews
and the Communist Party falls.

One aspect, then, of the complexity involved in the discussion
of the relationship between Jews and Communism is the variety
of types of Jews involved, and the many aspects of their existence that might be relevant to their relationship to Communism.
But then, if being Jewish means so many different things, what
does this do to the larger question of the relationship between
Jewishness and Communism? Define a man as "Jewish," and
then, it appears, one must interpret his behavior in terms of his
"Jewishness." But possibly some other factor, having no relation to his religio-cultural background—for example, occupation
—may explain his relationship to Communism. However, occupation, too, is affected by the historical experience of the group.
And, if so, when one speaks of the effect of occupation, does
one not also speak of the indirect effect of the religio-cultural
background, even though the person studied may not be aware
of it?

The relationship between occupation and religio-cultural background may be more complex than yet suggested, for if occupation does have some influence on political outlook and activity,
it may have such an effect only in the presence of some aspect

of the religio-cultural tradition. Perhaps the impact of the occupation may only be felt within a social sphere formed by a
concentration of people from the Jewish group who have entered
into that occupation, creating a special milieu in which it is
hard to differentiate the effect of occupation from that of religio-
cultural background.[5]

These complexities are raised only because it seems to me
that an intricate combination of religio-cultural background,
historical experience, and the special occupational history of
Jews in America explains why so many Communists were Jews.
All these factors, it will be seen, are part of the story.

This discussion operates on the basis of a common sociological definition of a Jew: someone who considers himself to be
at some times and in some way a Jew and who is so considered
by others. This is a somewhat formalistic definition. To give it
a content more important for present purposes, it can be said
that people in this category, no matter how diverse, have something in common. These common traits derive primarily from
the common history which most Jews, no matter of what type,
have experienced. Whether "non-Jewish" or "Jewish" Jews of
the second generation are considered, it will be found that their
fathers probably spoke the same language, engaged in the same
group of occupations, followed the same religion and customs,
emigrated at roughly the same time, from the same cultural
sphere, to the same country, settling in the same neighborhoods
in certain cities. This commonness of historical position means
that the ardent Zionist and the ardent Communist share something. This is a very minimal statement. In considering what it
is that they share, less agreement will be found. Do they share
a common character or personality, common values, a common
outlook? Perhaps, to some extent. However, there is no question

but that most Jews in this country share a common history of rapid rise in the socio-economic scale, and a common tendency to be more interested in liberal politics (to use this term as it is generally used in America, to refer to all political positions left of center or that have historically been derived from left-of-center positions).[6] They certainly shared other things, but this is enough to explain a good deal of the relationship between Jews and the American Communist Party.

During the twenties, the Jewish Federation, and later the Jewish Section, was one of the most important of the foreign-language groups in the Workers Party. However, it was no more important as a foreign-language section than the Russian Federation at the beginning of this period, or the Finnish Federation during the middle of the twenties. If we considered only the Yiddish-speaking element in the Communist Party, there would not be anything exceptional to explain. Just as other groups of workers from Eastern Europe had strong Left-Wing Socialist elements which turned Communist, so, too, did the Jews. In Chapter II it was pointed out that the Jewish group was the largest immigrant group in which the Communists had any important influence—much larger numerically than either the Russian, the Finnish, the Ukrainian, the Hungarian, or the South Slavic. In Chapter III it was pointed out, too, that the Jewish group had the peculiar fortune to be so concentrated in the clothing industries that Jewish Communists, as *Jewish* Communists, could and did play an important role in the labor movement without modifying their ethnic identification.

These two factors alone would have given the Jewish group a rather more prominent place in the Communist Party than some other ethnic elements. However, there were two other factors of some importance. First, the leadership, and perhaps a good part of the membership, of the Russian and Hungarian federations had a large Jewish component.[7] More important, a good part of the English-speaking Section of the party was also of Jewish origin, and some of its major leaders during the twenties were Jews. Lovestone and Gitlow were the two most prominent, but there were also William Weinstone, Bertram Wolfe, Jack Stachel, and many others.[8]

Thus from the beginning the Jews appeared in the Communist Party under two aspects: as immigrant, foreign-language-speaking workers, and as an assimilated, English-speaking element which did not particularly consider itself Jewish. Some leaders in the Russian and Hungarian federations were Jews who had, before emigration, become assimilated to the dominant cultures of their countries.

This double aspect of being "Jewish"—by identification and commitment, and by origin—explains some of the confusion that arises in discussing the role of Jews in the Russian Bolshevik Party. There were many individually prominent Jews in the party—most notably, Trotsky, Zinoviev, and L. B. Kamenev. But the Jewish (by commitment) socialists of Russia and Poland were for the most part anti-Bolshevik, and were organized in the party known as the Bund, which consistently supplied some of the strongest and most consistent anti-Communists in Europe and America.

In the United States, of course, assimilation did not quite mean what it meant in Czarist Russia. It was much more common—indeed, one might say very common among the immigrants and almost universal among their children—and it did not involve as much hostility to Jewish interests. In any case, both elements, the assimilated and the unassimilated, were prominent in the Communist Party.

As long as the party was predominantly working class and

strongly revolutionary in ideology, it appeared unlikely that it could make any inroads among the native-born Jewish group, because this group moved rapidly and almost completely out of the factories. To a group of white-collar workers, business people, salesmen, professionals, intellectuals, the Communist Party in the twenties, in its radical and revolutionary "third-period" phase, had little to offer. It might have been expected that with the waning of the significance of the foreign-language groups, the Communist Party would lose what color of Jewish predominance it carried in the twenties.

There is no evidence that the party's successes among the unemployed during the early thirties involved the Jewish unemployed more than the non-Jewish. There is evidence of important success in this period in bringing in (if not holding) Negroes, but, as far as can be told, there was no special impact on the Jewish group.[9] During this period, for example, there was no upsurge among the Communist Jewish garmentworkers. They were active, but they were never to achieve again the strength they displayed in the cloakmakers strike of 1926.

One pocket of strength among Jews did develop in the early thirties, and suggested the outline of the future. In City College, in New York, there grew up an active and important group of young Communists, which included John Gates, Joseph Starobin, Joseph Clark, Max Weiss, and others.

In the case of every other foreign-language group, the initial base of immigrant support was never greatly extended. Even when the party turned, after 1938, to an attempt to cultivate ethnic groups in this country, it operated on the basis of the attachments of the immigrant generation to language and to home country. The dynamic forces that had created an immigrant base for the Communist Party in America stemmed from the immigrant generation. Nothing new was added. The cadres were shifted around and new historical developments, such as the rise of Hitler and a new world war, aroused dormant sentiments.

In the case of the Jews, the matter was quite different. Here new dynamic tendencies came into play characteristic of the native-born second generation alone, and a whole new base for the Communist Party in America was created. This base consisted of the large numbers of Jews in the second generation who entered white-collar work and the professions, and, in particular, the quasi-professional occupations of teaching, social work, librarianship, and the like. In the rapid increase of white-collar workers and professionals in the party in the late thirties, the new elements were largely Jewish, of the second generation of Jews in this country.

At this point, the problem of social definition in the effort to achieve understanding becomes critical. Did the teachers and social workers and white-collar workers of this period in general turn to Communism? Or did the Jewish young men and women turning to these professions and occupations in large numbers find Communism attractive? The matter is not a simple one, and yet if we think in terms of an occupational group, we look for one set of determinants and explanations, and if we think in terms of an ethnic group, another. In fact, both must be kept in mind—the occupations involved and the characteristics of those who were being recruited into them.

At the end of 1935, after a struggle lasting for some years, the American Federation of Teachers, a national union, was captured by an alliance of Communists, Socialists, and other elements.[10] The New York branch, the Teachers Union, was fully dominated by the Communists. Now it would be ridiculous to say there was something about teaching in the Depression that turned people to Communism; the contrary would seem truer. While some teachers were fired, and some teachers had their salaries delayed, they fared better during the Depression than almost anyone else. The reductions in their salaries never quite matched the reduction in income of unprotected workers and businessmen, or of salaried white-collar personnel. They formed a group with relatively protected income at a time when prices were declining.

This was the economic situation of teachers *in general*. However, the A.F.T. did not represent teachers "in general." It represented a tiny proportion of the country's teachers who were organized in the union. About one quarter—later, one third—of its membership was in New York City. Other large groups of members were in Chicago and Philadelphia.[11] Obviously, it included a highly selected group of teachers, and the capture of the union by the Communists (leaving aside for the moment the fact that a large number of Communists was not needed for an efficient and hard-working fraction to capture a union) said nothing about the characteristics of teachers in general. As to the membership of the union, in New York at least, and very likely in Philadelphia and elsewhere, there were a sizable number of Jewish teachers in the union.[12] It is understandable that Jewish teachers might find unionism more attractive than other teachers. They came from a group that had created powerful trade unions, their immigrant fathers had been largely workers and members of trade unions, and it might well be expected that Jewish teachers would be more attracted to the idea of a teachers union than teachers coming from small-town, farming, white-collar, and other backgrounds.

In addition, the Jewish teachers might have felt most pinched during the Depression. They were just entering the teaching profession, in New York and other cities. Since they were entering under adverse circumstances, they often found themselves unemployed, were forced to take poorer positions, as substitutes, and found discrimination in their efforts to get better jobs. In the colleges, the Jewish faculty members faced the same difficulties, and often faced even more discrimination.

At the same time that some young Jewish men and women were turning to Communism, others were turning to Socialism. The years between 1930 and 1935 were almost as prosperous for the Socialist Party as for the Communist, and the Socialist Party drew on very much the same social base. Any one of a dozen little accidents might turn one young man to the militant Socialists, another to the Communists, a third to the Lovestone-ites—such things as who his friends were, where the local headquarters was located, what his father or his uncle had been, who ran the best (social) parties. The groups often found it easy to co-operate despite their deep and significant differences in political organization and attitude. In the early Depression, their leadership was more divided than their membership. It took a while for the peculiar cast of mind of Bolshevism to penetrate to the membership and for the specific Bolshevik pattern of matter-of-course lying and betrayals to disillusion the young Socialists and turn them from allies into enemies. In the meantime, there was a good deal of co-operation between young Jewish Socialists and Communists in the Teachers Union,[13] in various student organizations,[14] and in other areas of activity into which second-generation Jews were moving.

During the early years of the Depression, then, there were a number of tendencies working to produce groups of young Jewish radicals in white-collar and professional occupations: the movement of young Jews into such fields,[15] the difficulties they faced as newcomers in the Depression, and their greater familiarity with the range of radical positions and groups owing to family background and social surroundings in the Jewish sections of the large cities. Under these circumstances, was there, as so many believe, some relationship between certain intellectual occupations (teaching, social work, librarianship) and Communism? It has been argued that these occupations combine professional status and an intellectual milieu without the income and prestige that might make the members of these occupations supporters of the *status quo*.[16]

While the social origins of those filling these occupations must be disengaged from the occupational roles themselves, the occupational role does have some effect in leading to openness to radical ideas. Some weight does indeed have to be given to developments within these occupations that were quite independent, apparently, of the social origins of the newcomers entering them. During the early thirties, for example, there was a good deal of thinking about the relationship between education and social change, and various positions growing out of the progressive-education movement were argued at Teachers College, in New York. Particularly important were the "Frontier" thinkers, associated with the magazine *Social Frontier*.[17] This intellectual development, influenced by the Depression, had little to do with the Jewish background of the substitute and unemployed teachers of the early thirties who were active in the Teachers Union. While individual Jews may have played a role in developing new ideas as to the possible uses of education to improve society, these intellectual tendencies were quite independent of the development of the Jewish group in America. This type of thinking did help create a milieu in which young radical Jewish teachers found themselves at home.

Nevertheless, whatever the facilitating effect of the milieu of ideas in teaching in creating a basis for Communist successes, it was not of central importance, for in other fields, where there was no such thinking, there were similar successes. For example, as part of the movement of young, college-trained Jews into white-collar and professional employment, a sizable body of Jewish civil-service workers developed in New York. There was no advanced thinking by anyone at this time about the role of the civil service in building a progressive society; no parallel can be found in the civil service to the "Frontier" thinkers. There was, however, a parallel between the social characteristics of the new civil-service workers and the new teachers. And in the civil service in New York and some other large cities, without benefit of new ideological trends, small unions were formed, which eventually were merged into the State, County, and Municipal Workers of America, the United Federal Workers, and the United Public Workers. In these unions, as in the Teachers Union, there was the same conflict of different radical groups for leadership, and the same eventual predominance of the Communists.

The case of the social workers is perhaps most interesting for a disentangling of the relative significance of the social origins of individuals entering a field and the intellectual milieu of the field itself. There were very few social workers in this country at the onset of the Depression, and most of them worked for agencies supported by private philanthropy. The tradition that linked social work with reform still existed and had some strength, but competed with a newer orientation toward social work as a profession. In the early thirties, a "Rank-and-File" movement developed among social workers, first in New York City, among the employees of private agencies. It had a double aspect. First, it was interested in emphasizing the links of social work with social action and social change. And second, and somewhat later, it was interested in organizing social workers in trade-union form. The historian of this movement described the first Social Workers Discussion Club, organized in New York in the spring of 1931:

Seeking a clean break with both pessimism and feeble-minded amiability, the club put on its platform leaders of the unemployed, Communist editors, left-wing writers and union organizers—with this injunction: 'Tell us what you know. We know nothing. We're here to learn.' . . . New York endorsed the march of the unemployed to City Hall in 1932, contributed to the National Hunger March on Washington the same year, and voted endorsement of the Workers Unemployment Insurance Bill [all Communist-initiated actions].[18]

The Rank-and-File movement tried to establish "protective associations," that is, unions.[19] "Historically . . . the first protective association in the field of social work was the New York Association of Federation Workers [that is, workers of the agencies supported by the Federation of Jewish Philanthropies] . . . the example of New York was subsequently followed by workers in Jewish agencies in Brooklyn, Boston, Philadelphia and Detroit." [20] These protective associations of the Rank-and-File, beginning in the Jewish agencies, became the social-service unions of the Union of Office and Professional Workers of America in 1937. By 1939, they had organized 3,000 members, 65 per cent in New York City.[21] This organization may have contained a higher proportion of Communists than any other existing legitimate trade union. It was able to follow the Communist line in detail, and with relatively weak opposition from within the union. Efforts to fight the Communist leadership were met with expulsion. The leadership's attempts to fulfill party doctrine led to such demands as that the United Service for New Americans, which worked with incoming Jewish refugees, hire Negro caseworkers. And their power was such that this was done. One can only wonder what happened when a Yiddish-speaking Jew fresh from a displaced-persons camp confronted his Negro caseworker for the first time. The Jewish agencies finally rebelled in 1950 and 1951, and terminated their contracts, but it was only the outbreak of the Korean war and the increasingly severe pressure on Communists everywhere that gave them the courage to fight this powerful and obstreperous union.[22]

As in the case of the teachers, there is a complex question of interplay between ideological tendencies in the field of social work, responding to the enormous strains created by the Depression, and the social characteristics of new elements entering the field. The job of the social worker changed during the Depression, as it had already been changing before it. The mere fact that it was now a profession, a way of making a living based on special education, rather than a vocation that was appropriate for young upper-class and upper-middle-class men and women, attracted young Jewish men and women then attending college in large numbers and looking for new careers based on education. Its connection with social reform also made social work attractive. Entering it, these new recruits inevitably brought with them their predispositions—toward a radical interpretation of their work, toward unionization, toward casting the agencies in the role of exploiting employers and the professional worker in the role of exploited proletarian. Long hours and low wages —reflecting both the tradition of social work as a vocation for those who did not enter it primarily to make a living, and the increased pressures on social agencies because of the Depression—created conditions favorable to unionization. Yet it was the Jewish social workers that first organized unions. Just as among the teachers, there was a selective unionization, and a selective radicalization. In 1938, of 20,000 social workers in private agencies, only 2,000 were organized in the Left-Wing social-service employees' unions.[23] While organization under Communist leadership went further among social workers than among teachers, in neither case could it be said, simply, that teachers and social workers showed a tendency to become Communists or accept the leadership of Communist groups. There were some predisposing circumstances in some fields, but as important as the conditions affecting the field in general were the predispositions of many of those who were entering them in the early thirties.

Just as in the industrial trade unions described in the last chapter, there were two phases in the development of Communist influence within professional and white-collar groups. During the early period, until about 1935, small groups of Communist activists formed and fought, for trade unions and for dominance over other radical and nonradical elements within them. Victories created a solid corps, "tested in battle," and an organization that was Communist-dominated. Then a period of "mass membership" followed the first victories. Thus, a delegate to the New York State Convention in 1938, a member of the Teachers Union, reported: [24]

Local No. 5 [New York] . . . has grown from about 300 about three years ago to 7,000 today. We also helped set up W.P.A. and College Teachers locals of 1,000 each; and in addition, seven locals upstate. . . . During this time, our fraction of 35 grew to many hundreds. . . . This is a big fraction and more than is necessary in our industry, if you wish to call it that. I think about 100 or so would be sufficient to work within the union; and so we have sent our Party members into the apparatus of our Party everywhere, in the Counties, in the Sections, and in the District. You fall over teachers everywhere.[25]

Frank Meyer, a party functionary in Chicago around the same time, describes social workers there in much the same way—there were far more than were required to work within social-work groups and unions, and more than enough to spare.[26]

There were also small groups of doctors, lawyers, and dentists in the party, which again were part of the upsurge in middle-class membership during the late thirties. As with teachers, social workers, and civil-service workers, it is difficult to make any effective argument that they moved into the Communist Party because something in their occupational role or in their socio-economic position during the Depression years predisposed them to radicalism. The development of such groups in the party is largely to be explained in terms of the ethnic origin of those being recruited into these professions in the twenties and thirties. Many second-generation Jews then moved into these occupations.[27] The doctors and lawyers in the Communist Party were no random sample of doctors and lawyers in general, but were predominantly drawn from these newcomers. Certainly they suffered the fate of newcomers—difficulties in establishing practices, making a decent living, achieving status.[28] The fact that some of them joined the Communist Party may be explained with equal justice in terms of the special difficulties of new-comers in an occupational role, with the accompanying frus-trations and resentment, or in terms of the ethnic background which may have made radical politics familiar to them, and thus made them more accessible to Communist influence. In either case, very much the same people were involved; the doctors and dentists and lawyers in the Communist Party were generally Jewish doctors, dentists, and lawyers.

To suggest the order of magnitude of these groups in the party, there were twenty to thirty of each in Chicago in the late thirties, out of a membership of about 4,000.[29] There were thirty Communist lawyers in Los Angeles in 1948-49.[30] Herbert A. Philbrick says that there were eighty members in professional groups of the Communist Party in Boston in the years after World War II (the professional group contained all those higher professionals whose membership in a regular unit might badly affect their opportunities to earn a livelihood, and included almost all doctors and lawyers, as well as some college teachers, engineers, writers, and the like). Philbrick also asserts that during the same years there were 2,000 members in professional groups throughout the party. In sum, there may have been a couple of hundred lawyers and a couple of hundred doctors who became members of the Communist Party.[31] It is generally believed by the knowledgeable that Communist dentists were more common than lawyers or doctors.

I have argued that the development of a large white-collar and professional membership in the Communist Party in the middle and late thirties and the rise of a large Jewish, second-generation membership during the same period were, in effect, two aspects of the same phenomenon. While I feel these two aspects were for the most part related, it is also true that many non-Jewish middle-class and professional people joined the party and that, on the other side, many working-class Jews also came into the party during this period. Indeed, in the late thirties and in the forties, the party was big enough and strong enough to attract many different kinds of people. In the later thirties and during the war, people of all kinds and all backgrounds might be found in the party. We speak here of major trends only, and large numbers of people were outside them.

One basis for the appeal of Communism to newly middle-class Jews has been suggested: the rapid rise of this group into white-collar and professional employment, leading, as a general pattern, to the existence of a good deal of resentment of the difficulties for latecomers of establishing a solid base. A second basis for this pattern has been suggested, too, and that is the general liberal and, in part, socialist orientation of American

Jews, leading to their greater accessibility and lower resistance to Communist appeals. A variety of other explanations rather different from these two can be put forward to explain this phenomenon of the relationship between the Jewish second generation and Communism. Communist policy toward, first, professional and middle-class groups and, second, Jews and Jewish questions changed radically in the middle thirties and even more radically after the German invasion of Russia. Certainly it became easier for both middle-class people and Jews, and thus middle-class Jews, to become members of the Communist Party.

It is scarcely necessary to document the remarkable change that came over the party as the threat of Hitler frightened Stalin.[32] A strong effort was made to change the image and reality of the Communist Party from that of a group meeting in small conspiratorial units to one organized somewhat more like a legitimate political organization and thus more "catholic." Instead of the special Communist organization into districts and sections, a new form of organization, based on states, counties, and other areas corresponding to American political organization was introduced. While not universal, this new organization did come into effect in those areas with the densest memberships (for example, New York State). The size of membership units was increased.[33] It was probably true, as the party organizational expert F. Brown wrote, that "The American workers that join our ranks will feel much better, will feel at home, in a unit of 50 or 60 that meets in a hall than in a small unit of 10 or 13 crowded in a bedroom, sitting on the beds and floor." [34] There may be some question whether the dingy halls were really more attractive than the crowded bedrooms to white-collar and professional people, but in time, the Communist clubs, paralleling the structure of Democratic and Republican clubs, made it easier for the ordinary run of white-collar and professional people to feel more at home in the party.

The party propaganda was also suddenly muted; violent revolution became the esoteric doctrine, collective security and the support of the New Deal the exoteric doctrine. The demands on party workers were reduced. As Browder wrote, "We must abolish that sectarian nonsense which thinks that when a worker joins the party he must give up all family life." [35] Also abandoned, at least publicly, was the notion that the working classes were the only worthy elements from which the party might recruit. It was generally the case that in the "Left" periods the emphasis was on recruiting workers and Negroes, in the "Right" periods everybody.[36] And 1935-39 and 1941-45 were "Right" periods.

From 1935 on, *everyone* was to be appealed to. Browder, in speaking about infiltrating other organizations, wrote: "This applies to every kind of organization. It applies especially to Negro organizations, church organizations of all kinds, Parent-Teachers Associations, every kind of organization, including Republican and Democratic neighborhood clubs, Townsend organizations, Epic and Utopian and all the rest. . . ." [37] Special attention was now paid to the urban middle-class elements. Indeed, one finds a new heading in a "Report to the National Agitation and Propaganda Conference, January 18, 1935" using just this term: "Urban Middle-Class Elements." From then on, party directives on organization and concentration urged members not to ignore "militant, progressive forces among the . . . middle-class generally, among intellectuals and professional people. . . ." [38]

Around this time, special professional units were organized. The ordinary white-collar workers would be part of their regular street units or branches, or part of shop groups. Professionals, too, might be part of such units. But in the case of those professionals who might feel uncomfortable in a regular unit, a special professional unit could be created. A report from Detroit in July 1937 asserts that twenty-eight of 226 units were professional.[39] Special attention was now given to the problems of professionals, and William Z. Foster asserted: "Special organizational forms must be developed for this work. We now have many professional units, and in some cases, sections of professionals. We are also cultivating various organizations of professionals." [40] Signs that the professionals in the party were at least superficially influencing the old Bolsheviks can even be detected. It is somewhat startling to read in an article by Henry Winston on the Young Communist League, "It is important for our branch leaders to study such books as Grace Coyle's *Studies in Group Behavior* and Clara Kaiser's *Objectives of Group Work.*" [41]

During the period of the Nazi-Soviet pact, there was a brief check in this development, but after the German attack on Russia, the party returned with enthusiasm to the development of a middle-class form of organization. The units grew larger and larger, attendance and involvement declined. With the organization of the Communist Political Association in 1944, the old types of Communist organization almost disappeared. John Williamson complained: "We cannot be satisfied with a situation in which in large clubs of 200 to 600 members, only 25 per cent are in attendance or participate in discussions or elections. . . . We see clubs reaching the size of 500 to 700. . . . Experience has shown that only a few clubs with a membership of 500 function with maximum effectiveness . . . the majority . . . are more effective with a maximum membership of 300." [42] With the reconstitution of the party, one of the first points to be changed was the system of organization in large clubs; their size was to be reduced, and the more Bolshevik term of "branches" now applied to them.[43]

What was the impact of this ten years of "liberalism" (aside from the pact interlude) on the relation between the Communist Party and middle-class groups? The interest in the professional and intellectual and middle-class groups reflected the new line and the new emphasis on public relations and influencing opinion. The Popular Front period did facilitate a great increase in the party's influence and membership among the white-collar and professional groups. But when the party hardened after 1945 and the end of Browderism, there was no significant decline in the middle-class part of the party's membership. In fact, the party had perhaps its greatest success with middle-class, professional, and intellectual groups during the Wallace campaign. Only government attack by way of Smith Act trials, the Korean war, and the party's own extreme reaction to these led to the rapid decline of the middle-class membership after 1950. The middle-class elements stuck to the party as well as any other group. Of course, by 1950-51, a good part of them felt trapped by previous activity, the virulence of public reaction, the difficulty of dissociation without danger.

The party's position on white-collar and middle-class groups facilitated their entry, but it was also a response to their entry as well as a cause of it.

What, then, of the party's point of view and position on specifically Jewish issues? On occasion, the party took certain positions on Jewish issues which were attractive to Jews, but in general there was no group in the population for which the party showed more contempt and disdain, in its formulations of specific party positions, than the Jews. Melech Epstein has told the incredible story of the party's treatment of the Arab

massacres of Jews in Palestine in 1929. This was initially referred to in the Yiddish *Freiheit* as a "pogrom." The party then
severely castigated the *Freiheit* for not seeing the Arab uprising
as a "class war . . . against British imperialism and their
Zionist agents." The *Freiheit* immediately corrected its error by
resorting to a treatment of the Palestine events not very different
from that of an anti-Semitic newspaper—indeed, the cartoons
it ran of hook-nosed and bloated Jews sadistically attacking
Arabs could have appeared in any German anti-Semitic newspaper. The events of the twenties had already produced an un-
bridgeable gap between the Jewish labor movement and the
Communists; the 1929 events estranged the rest of the community.[44]

From this point on, it was a rare legitimate Jewish organization that was anything but anti-Communist. All the central
religious bodies (Orthodox, Conservative, Reform), the defense
organizations (American Jewish Committee, American Jewish
Congress, Anti-Defamation League), the Zionist organizations,
the community fund-raising organizations were anti-Communist.
The old Yiddish-speaking Communist base remained immune
to the almost unanimous opposition of Jewish communal organizations, for all the reasons immigrant organizations sturdily
manage to survive until the immigrant generation has died out.
But this Jewish communal opposition did not prevent the Communists, as has been seen, from establishing a powerful base
in the second generation of Jews, the rising middle-class. The
reasons for this are to be found in the general estrangement of
this generation from traditional Jewish values and institutions.
Only a small part of this generation in the thirties, for example,
was attached to the synagogues. Only a small part was Zionist.
This part was, of course, staunchly anti-Communist. As for the

rest, the indifference of the Communists to any specific Jewish issue meant nothing to it.[45]

There was one Jewish issue on which the Communists could take a positive stand: the question of anti-Semitism. Czarist Russia had been anti-Semitic; Communist Russia banned anti-Semitism. America had anti-Semitism, which was (to Communists) inevitably associated with capitalism. Hitler's Germany, the sworn enemy of the Soviet Union, was anti-Semitic. On this issue, then, if not on Zionism and Jewish religion, both outlawed and oppressed in the Soviet Union, the Communist Party could make itself attractive to all Jews, and particularly to those rising young professionals who found in anti-Semitism a strong bar to their upward rise. Interestingly enough, the party found it unnecessary to make any important issue of this; not a single article in *The Communist* of the thirties or forties dealing with anti-Semitism can be found. There is a great deal of writing about anti-Semitism in the agitational party press addressed to Jews. But in the theoretical organ, giving guidance on party problems, it was apparently never necessary to explain to party workers and Jewish party workers how the party should handle an issue like anti-Semitism. It was taken for granted that no special appeal was necessary to the Jewish group. In contrast, there were literally scores of articles on the proper approach to the Negroes, the handling of Negro issues, the theoretical understanding of the Negro position.

The party theoretical organ did carry an occasional article to keep the Jewish party members "straight" on Zionism. The Jewish Bureau of the Pittsburgh District raised in 1936 the question of "whether the emphasis as to the *main danger* [in Palestine] . . . should not be placed on British imperialism, which should be charged with the *whole* responsibility for the Palestine happenings." The party answered: The main enemy is British

imperialism *backed by Zionism*. We must not let up the attack
on Zionism, despite the endangering of the United Front with
Jewish organizations.[46]

The party was unquestionably aided in its appeal to Jews in
general and liberal-minded Jews in particular by its strong opposition to Nazi Germany and its participation in the Spanish war.
Certainly many Jews were brought into the party because of
their deep concern for these issues. Many more were brought
into front groups such as the American League for Peace and
Democracy. But if they were brought into the party on these
issues, they remained for other reasons. They soon became Communists, if they did not enter as such. When the Nazi-Soviet
pact was signed, the party was shaken, but the Jewish part of
the party seemed hardly more shaken than the others. No important group of Jewish leaders left. (Melech Epstein lists three
party members and two sympathizers.[47]) When, in August 1940,
Roy Hudson reported that there had been only a 15-per-cent
drop in the registration for that year, he also pointed out that
the loss was no greater in New York than in the rest of the
party.[48]

During the war, the only concern of the Communist Party was
the defense of the Soviet Union. It then had the great luck of
not having to attack British imperialism and the Jewish community in Palestine, for both were aiding the Soviet fatherland.
For a brief period, its isolation from the Jewish community was
somewhat broken. The Jewish People's Fraternal Order, a
section of the large and powerful Communist fraternal society,
the International Workers Order, was accepted as an affiliate of
the American Jewish Congress in 1944. Certain sections of the
American Jewish Congress were successfully penetrated by the
Communists, for a few years released from the necessity of
denouncing Zionism as a British (or American) imperialist

plot. During the war, an American Jewish Conference was set up by the major Jewish organizations to represent the point of view of American Jews in the postwar settlement, and under the prevailing glow of unity, the J.P.F.O. was admitted also into that organization. But the Jewish Labor Committee, inveterate enemies of the Communists, and the American Jewish Committee then withdrew, and the Communist victory in getting the J.P.F.O. accepted as a legitimate part of the Jewish community during the special conditions of wartime was a short-lived one.[49]

The new benign Communist line on Palestine survived briefly the abandonment of Browderism and the opening of the cold war. There had, of course, been "errors," but in October 1945, Alexander Bittelman, the chief Communist Jewish theoretician, could still write of Palestine that "it has become an important settlement of 600,000 souls, having developed a common national economy, a growing national culture, and the first elements of Palestinian Jewish statehood and self-government." [50] A year later, an important resolution on "Work Among the Jewish Masses" was adopted by a conference of Jewish party workers. While it attacked the error of having used the Zionist slogan of a "Jewish National Homeland in Palestine," and insisted on a joint Arab-Jewish attack on British imperialism, it did accept as a legitimate slogan "A National Homeland for the Jews in Palestine"—that is, national independence for the Jews, in cooperation with the Arabs, already in Palestine. And Bittelman, introducing the resolution, emphasized: "In the past, American Jewish Marxists have not always displayed a positive attitude to the rights and interests of the Jewish people, to the special needs and problems of our own American Jewish national group, and to the interests and rights of the Jewish Community in Palestine." [51]

The Communists were unable to adopt the position of the

majority of American Jews on Palestine. Thus, they never came out for free immigration into Palestine, because the Soviet Union opposed this even when friendliest to the Palestinian Jews. Nevertheless, the Communists managed for a while to maintain their position in the Zionist-oriented American Jewish Congress. Not that anyone was being fooled: [52] Zionists were accepting support from anyone who offered it; Communists held on to whatever community positions they had managed to attain in the glow of 1944. Then suddenly the Soviet Union supported partition and a Jewish state. The ever-versatile Bittelman now explained how *this* position (previously Marxist anathema) had become the true "Marxist" position (simply that the Soviet Union was now for it), and greeted the new Jewish state, reassuring the comrades who had difficulty in seeing the progressive nature of the struggle for Jewish statehood in Palestine.[53]

This brief period when the Soviet Union smiled on a Jewish Palestine helped Leo Isaacson win a special election for Congress in the Bronx in February 1948, and encouraged the illusion that Wallace might do well.[54] The honeymoon lasted through the 1948 national election, and perhaps helped Wallace pull a sizable Jewish vote.[55] By March 1949, A. B. Magil was already warning of the danger of the new state being sucked into the American imperialist whirlpool.[56] In 1949, the J.P.F.O. was thrown out of the American Jewish Congress. Communists remained entrenched in local areas, however, and in 1951 the Congress had to dissolve its Manhattan Division to get rid of them.[57]

The brief period when Communists could be positively "Jewish" was over in early 1949. At the end of 1948, the Yiddish newspapers and Jewish institutions of the Soviet Union were suddenly closed, the leading Jewish writers of the Soviet Union disappeared, and, as was later discovered, were shot or died in exile. The worst wave of anti-Semitism since the death of Hitler was directed at Soviet Jewry.[58] In May 1950, the Jewish Communists, apparently disturbed by these events (though not a word about them had appeared in the Communist Jewish press, Yiddish or English), were called together and sharply taken to task by John Williamson. Now, the November 1946 resolution which had called for a National Homeland for the Jews already in Palestine was denounced as a reflection of bourgeois nationalism. "Many comrades in Jewish work and in the *Morning Freiheit* have demonstrated great ideological weakness . . . and some have themselves fallen victim to the ravings of the bourgeoisie about 'What happened to the Jewish writers?' Such comrades must be sharply criticized. It is the opinion of the National Committee that comrades in the *Morning Freiheit* should work out a series of projects for self-correction. . . ." [59]

This time not a single Jewish leader is known to have left the party. The Jewish cadre remained solid. It seems obvious that the explanation for the attachment of Jewish Communists to the party must be found elsewhere than in the Communist positions on Jewish questions. Sometimes these positions brought in sympathizers, sometimes they repelled them. These positions sometimes made life and agitation and infiltration easier, sometimes they made it harder. But they are not primary to understanding the relationship between Jews and Communism.

Another line of party policy is of importance in efforts to understand the characteristics of party membership in the late thirties and forties, and specifically the middle-class and Jewish membership. This was the party policy on national groups.

Until the early thirties, the language groups, as previously discussed, were viewed by the party leaders as hindrances to the extension of the party's power in the working class. During the

strike and trade-union activities of the mid-thirties, and particularly in the C.I.O. drive in steel, they were viewed as aids in
the party's work in penetrating the working class. But until
about 1937, they were evaluated largely in terms of their significance in helping the party to reach the working class or hurting
the effort. As the language groups declined in significance in the
party in the early and middle thirties, there was less and less
discussion of their problems. There were still, of course, party
fractions in immigrant organizations, but there was little direct
attention to their potential role in helping or hurting the party.[60]

The new Popular Front policy—in which every group, no
matter what its "class character," might be enlisted to help the
Communist Party in aiding the Soviet Union—suggested that a
new approach to the old immigrant groups might be possible.
In June 1937, Earl Browder, in a report to a plenary meeting
of the Central Committee, announced an important new direc-
tion in policy. "For many years," he said, "we have spoken of
the need of a special approach to the problems of various strata
and groups of the population, if we want to build our Party
among them. A uniform, stereotyped propaganda and agitation
will always miss the mark with the majority of people, because
the majority is made of special groups. The general program
must be linked up with the particular problems of particular
groups." He then went on to discuss the special problems of
women, youth, Negroes, and farmers. But the fullest discussion
was devoted to what he now labeled "national groups." He said:

Finally, we have those many national groups in the communities—
what we have been accustomed to call our language work, thus
stressing only one side of a complicated problem. Our press and organization work among these national communities is stagnant.
This is giving rise to false theories about the dying out of the communities due to lack of new immigration and the Americanization
of the second and third generations. But we find that Americaniza-

tion does not disperse these communities. The second generation of Italian-Americans, for example, are just as proud of the first part of that hyphenated name as of the second. A glaring light is thrown on this question when nationalist and fascist propaganda from their home countries grip the second generation deeper than the original immigrants. . . . To engage them in the American class struggle . . . it is necessary to smash through the sectarian isolation of our national bureaus and national press; to throw them into the center of the community life; to utilize its national traditions, issues, and peculiarities; to appeal to its national pride and culture, to find thus the road to Americanization, Americanization in our understanding of the word; and, especially, to utilize the lessons of the blossoming of the nationalities under socialism in the Soviet Union. . . . Our special committee on this question at this Plenum must give us material for directing a far-reaching change, the beginning of a forward march among the national group, especially among the largest and most important ones, the Italians, Germans, Jews, Poles and Irish.[61]

The sharpness of this turn was indicated in the fact that at the Ninth Convention of the party, held in June 1936, there was no reference to the foreign-language groups at all, negative (as in the Eighth Convention, 1934) or positive.[62] In July 1937, the new line was presaged in an article by Israel Amter which urged specialized appeals to national groups in the New York elections.[63] At the Tenth Convention, in 1938, all the stops were pulled out. Browder's report even "extend[ed] the hand of brotherly cooperation to the Catholics"—how else was one to penetrate the impenetrable Irish population, the hardly less-impenetrable Italian, Polish, and German groups? [64] The party resolutions asserted: "This convention raises before the entire Party the urgent necessity of speedily effecting a decisive turn in all phases of Party recruiting and mass work among the *national groups and organizations,* in the first place among the Italians, Poles, Jews, South Slavs, and Spanish-speaking peoples.

The National Bureaus of the National Committee and the editorial staffs of the language press must be carefully examined, renewed, strengthened, and all sectarian tendencies overcome." [65] Now "sectarian" was used to refer not to the tendency for a group to emphasize its national culture, but, quite the contrary, to the tendency of Communists of immigrant background to *refuse* to emphasize it!

In August 1938, Amter expounded the new line at length, placing specific emphasis on the second, third, and fourth generations. "When we think of the second, third and fourth generations of the immigrants in this country as being absorbed in American life, we must not forget . . . that they are also essentially a part of the national group community and susceptible to nationalist propaganda. . . ." [66] The party was kept on course with long articles on the subject by Irene Browder (Mrs. Earl Browder) during 1938 and 1939. [67]

This policy received no check, but was only redirected, when the pact period cut off the major theme of antifascist unity which had been used in the national group work. Instead of appealing to groups on the basis of their opposition to Hitler, appeals were now directed to groups that favored isolationism, such as the Irish. The March 1940 resolution of the party called for "Solidarity with the Irish People," and Louis Budenz and Elizabeth Gurley Flynn were called upon to utilize their Irish background for the party. [68] This special appeal to the Irish had little success. Russia entered the war, and the party national group work again took up the more fruitful line of antifascist unity. [69]

What was the effect of this new line, beginning in 1937, in actually recruiting people on the basis of group allegiance and response to ethnic-group appeals? This is, naturally, difficult to estimate. In the Jewish group, one immediate effect was to create an atmosphere in which an emphasis on Jewish culture and Jewish national interests could flourish. When it is realized that even such a matter as a fund-raising drive for Jewish schools required higher party authority in the early thirties (any fund-raising might reduce funds available for more important party purposes), the importance of such a more-favorable atmosphere can be seen. The Yiddish schools of the International Workers Order, originally looked on askance as a remnant of chauvinism, were able to grow.[70] In 1944, when this policy of emphasizing the special interests of national groups was perhaps at its peak, the West Side Club of the Communist Political Association called off meetings for the Jewish holidays, and the I.W.O. published a history of the Jews in America that could have appeared under the imprint of a non-Communist Jewish organization.[71]

In 1942, the emphasis on the English-speaking second generation was increased by a shift in I.W.O. policy, which took the English-speaking out of the general lodges, and grouped them with the ethnic divisions of the fraternal order, as English-speaking sections. Thus, in 1945, some 10,000 of 45,000 members of the Jewish-American Section of the I.W.O. were in these English-speaking lodges.[72]

This new policy of national-group emphasis was possibly more successful among Slavic groups than among the Jewish. Communist influence grew among the Jews during the war; it grew at least as much among the Slavic groups. In the American Slavic Congress, the Communists had one of their most important fronts, and one which was also successful in moving out from the first-generation immigrant base into second-generation, English-speaking groups. The old pattern of Communist influence that was found in the twenties, however, still held with minor variations. Croatian and Slovene elements, rather than Serbian, and Czech and Slovak elements, rather than Polish, responded to the Communist-organized American Slav

Congress. Catholic influence and long-ingrained distrust of Russia kept the Poles away from Communist influence. But in the other Slavic communities, and in the Hungarian and Rumanian communities, the Communists flourished—sometimes with American government support of Communist-dominated "unity" groups because of their new status as allies. Their long-time opponents in the immigrant communities were now not only "reactionaries," but "Fascists," and enemies of the United States—or so it could be claimed, and often with some justice.[73]

In the Jewish and some Slavic groups, there was some success in reaching the second generation on the basis of a national-group appeal. And in these groups we find native-born Communists in national-group work.[74] From 1941 on, there was occasional emphasis on the importance of recruiting native-born members into work among national groups—an interesting reversal of emphasis from the early thirties.[75] From 1945 on, important functionaries born in this country directed national-group work: from 1945 to 1948, Steve Nelson; after 1948, Arnold Johnson.[76]

The party did not shift from this path. Despite the expulsion of Browder and the violent attack on and reversal of many of his policies, the Browderite emphasis on appeal to national groups remained—indeed, if anything, it became stronger.[77] And the party maintained its strong position among a number of ethnic groups through the forties. Thus, the South Slavic base, extended during the war, continued to grow, and in 1947, the largest Croatian fraternal union was captured.[78] And the Jewish ethnic base remained firm; the old Yiddish-speaking Communists had stuck to the party. The South Slavic party members, too, survived the attack on Tito in 1949. At that time, the Yugoslav Embassy had developed strong influence in the South Slavic communities, and Tito was idolized among South Slavic Communists. It might have been expected that Communists among American Croats and Slovenes would break with the Cominform and bring their newspapers and institutions into the Titoist fold. This was not the case. After a period of confusion, the major part ended on Stalin's side.

The South Slavs, like the Jews in the party, if they stayed long enough, were Bolshevized—or "Leninized" or "Stalinized." They might use national appeals to extend their influence in their ethnic communities, when the party line called for it. They could use these periods to gain recruits, and to win influence over sympathetic organizations. When the line then turned against the national interest, the cadre withdrew, relatively unharmed, taking along with it its recruits, and sometimes, if its organizational work had been done well enough, the organizations that had been captured.

In the 1950's, as trade-union and professional and middle-class members left the party or were expelled, the party partially reverted to its character of the twenties, when the most effective appeal was directed to the foreign-speaking and the foreign-born. For as the cold war grew in intensity, the party found it less and less possible to present itself to major strata of the American population as an "American" party, as the patriotic party it had been during the Popular Front and World War II. It directed its appeals to those groups in the population that it thought were discontented with and unhappy in America—the Negroes and, in lesser degree, foreign-language groups. In the fifties, it was, in effect, a quasi-treasonable organization, supporting the enemies of this country, and it appealed to the discontented.

Thus, as the party membership shrank, as newspapers and organizations were abandoned, the party withdrew more and more to the ethnic islands which had been the first basis of its support. Communist foreign-language dailies continued to be published after the English *Daily Worker* was abandoned— just as they had existed before it was founded. The foreign-language members in the party shared in the general decline, but since they were somewhat isolated, socially and linguistically and by age, from the main stream of American public opinion, the rate of their defection was low. Perhaps, too, some of them clung to the party in fear, for many had been members of the International Workers Order and other organizations now judged subversive, many had never become citizens, many were being deported and others feared deportation and separation from their families. The party presented itself as the great defender of the rights of the foreign-born. But in the later forties and the fifties, the foreign-language groups offered few advantages to the party. They had shrunk in size, they no longer dominated the working forces of heavy industry, they were aged. Their only virtue for the Communists was that they were faithful.

In 1956, when Nikita Khrushchev and official Communist organs admitted that Stalin had indeed been a bloodthirsty dictator, that Jewish culture in the Soviet Union had been wiped out, and that Jews had lived in fear, the entire party was badly shaken, and the Jewish members of the party were more shaken than the rest. Many of the second-generation members who had joined in the early thirties, and stuck to the party through purge and pact, now broke away. In the party fight that developed between the faction led by John Gates, editor of the *Daily Worker*—one of this generation—and the old Bolshevik faction of Foster, the second-generation Jewish members seemed more sympathetic to Gates, and a large proportion of them left the party during the fight and after his defeat.[79] Whether they acted this way because they were particularly affected by the fact that they had been fed lies as to the fate of the Jews in the Soviet Union for eight years or because as intellectuals they were capable of feeling and responding to the enormities revealed in Khrushchev's speech more strongly than other elements in the party, it would be hard to say.

But whereas many of the group of native-born Jewish intellectuals left the party, the older Yiddish-speaking members shuddered briefly and continued firm. Despite the fact that Yiddish culture had been for many years the chief point with which they argued the virtues of the Soviet Union with non-Communists of the immigrant generation, they did not break. The *Daily Worker* was liquidated in the aftermath to Khrushchev's speech, but the *Daily Freiheit* continued.[80] For the older Communists, the immigrant generation, the Communist world was their entire life, and it was a case of "even if ye slay me, I will remain faithful." And indeed, they remained faithful though scores of Yiddish poets and writers and musicians, their pride through three decades, had been secretly executed. Their children were somewhat more flexible, and were still capable of being disillusioned.

The year of Khrushchev's speech, of the brief acknowledgment of the fate of Yiddish culture in the Soviet Union, and of the crushing of the Hungarian revolution almost destroyed the Communist Party in the United States. The Jewish issue was only one among a number capable of disillusioning the hardest cadreman that year. There was, it appears, a disproportionate withdrawal from the party after 1956 of the second-generation Jewish members who still remained after the hard years of the earlier fifties, but I cannot conclude, on the basis of the whole history of the thirties, forties, and fifties, that the Communist position on specific Jewish questions, or on national and ethnic groups in general, played any major role in gaining and keeping for many years the adherence of a large number of Jewish members.

There is one aspect of Communist history in the thirties and forties that has not yet been discussed and which is most important to an understanding of the relationship between American Jews and Communism. This is the party's general success in the intellectual community.[81]

I will not enter the dispute as to the extent and nature of Communist influence among writers, artists, composers, actors, directors, script-writers, and the like. But it was great, from the early thirties on. It is important to keep in mind this large, loose grouping of intellectuals and cultural figures which surrounded the Communist Party for twenty years. Young Jews were strongly attracted to these fields of culture, easily influenced by the successful in them, and the large number of Communists in these areas played an important role for them in making Communism respectable, acceptable, something to be taken seriously.

The attraction between a part of the intellectual and cultural groups and Communism is world-wide. It has been discussed by many writers, and at great length. It is part, clearly enough, of the long-term romance that has attached the major part of the intelligentsia to the Left. The general explanations for this phenomenon are well known. Freed from the restraints of conservative and traditional thinking, the intelligentsia finds it easier to accept revolutionary thinking, which attacks the established order of things in politics, religion, culture, and society. That its opposition to the established society it knows leads the intelligentsia to the support of another established society that is far more brutal, more deadening to culture, and a ferocious enemy of freedom is another matter. I take as given this great influence of Communism in intellectual and cultural circles; [82]

and this influence played an enormous role in bringing the second generation of Jews, attracted to intellect, enamored of culture, into the Communist Party.

Whatever it is that affected intellectuals, also affected Jews. They, too, looked with a cold and hostile eye on the world of received things, traditional religion, traditional culture, the traditional order of society. All these had historically meant for Jews oppression, anti-Semitism, restriction. Freedom and fraternity and human possibility were for them bound up with the breaking of old forms and the letting in of anything new and radical. Werner Cohn has given the best account of the permanent Jewish estrangement from the Right, the permanent attachment to the Left—an attachment to which the Communists became a partial heir.

Looking at the nineteenth century in Europe, he writes:

No Conservative Party in Europe—from the bitterly hostile Monarchists in Russia . . . to the amiable Tories of England—could reconcile itself to full Jewish political equality. Jews supported the Left . . . not only because they had become unshakeable partisans of the Enlightenment, but because they had no choice; as far as the internal life of the Right was concerned, the Emancipation [of the Jews] had never taken place, and the Christian religion remained a prerequisite for political participation. . . .

Radical Leftism . . . was the only political movement since the days of the Roman Empire in which Jews could become the spiritual brethren of non-Jews . . . radicalism could successfully challenge the spiritual hegemony of Christianity among broad layers of the population . . . radical Leftism—eschatological Socialism in particular—began to constitute itself as a new religious faith in which no separation between the sacred and profane occurred . . . the religious distinctions between Christians and Jews became totally irrelevant in the new faith. Here, from the point of view of the Jews, is the . . . decisive difference between the intellectual and dynamic aspects of Leftism [that is, between liberalism and radicalism]; the former offered them a wholly rational and superficial admission to the larger society; the latter involved a measure of real spiritual communion. . . .[83]

I do not think anyone has come closer to the heart of the matter than has the author of these paragraphs. The Jews did not join the party because of a rational economic interest. They joined out of faith. The party always believed that self-interest was decisive in leading it to power. But what could the party offer Americans, even if they were immigrants, industrial workers, Jews, Negroes? It could offer them a community, based on a faith in which all were equal. To be a Communist meant to shed the limitations of one's social reality, and to join in a fraternity that transcended the divisions of the world. This was the attraction of Communism to many Jews who no longer thought of themselves in any way as Jewish. And for many, faith remained stronger than interest.

FIVE · NEGROES AND THE PARTY

T he Communist Party devoted
more resources, more attention, more effort, to the recruitment
of Negro members than it expended on any other social group,
except perhaps for industrial workers and trade-unionists.[1] The
winning of Negro members was a constant theme in Communist Party work, emphasized in every other type of recruitment. The party wanted not only workers, but Negro workers;
not only youth, but Negro youth; not only women, but Negro
women. The party was not satisfied with a representation of
Negroes paralleling their proportion in the population in general. For the Negroes were the most oppressed part of the
population. Lenin himself, with his masterful capacity to focus
on those parts of the population where resentment and hatred
might be greatest, had decided that the Negroes were very important for the American Communist Party.[2] And Stalin, too,
the expert on the national question, was interested in the American Negro: he was the chief architect of the self-determination
line under which the party was expected to win American
Negroes to Communism and revolution.[3]

But during the twenties, the party showed little interest in the Negro as a potential recruit. The great majority of Negroes were still in the South, totally subjected and without political rights, and the Negro population of the North, which had increased during World War I, remained, despite some political activity and some success, in the quiescence that Americans then considered normal for Negroes.[4] It was the Comintern in Moscow that kept on directing the party to Negro work in the twenties, and it was its requests for Negroes on delegations, for Negroes to be trained in the new Communist schools in Moscow, that helped create what pressure there was to find and recruit Negroes into the party.[5]

Between 1928 and 1930, the Comintern hammered out a major new policy for the American Communist Party. The party was to campaign among the Negroes on the basis of the Negro "right to national self-determination" in the southern parts of the United States. The new line coincided with the onset of the Depression. Money and organizers were thrown into the field with a lavish hand, in both the South and the North, and for the first time the Negro membership of the party began to rise. The appeal to Negroes, the most oppressed and potentially the most radical segment of the population (according to Communist theory), rises in Left periods, is muted in Right periods. In the early thirties, the so-called "third period," the Leftism of the Communist Party was most unrestrained.

Even in that radical era, the self-determination policy did not play any major role in work among the Negroes. The Communists used more characteristic and more effective tactics. They showed themselves as the one element in American life that demanded the goal that even Negro political organizations hesitated to put forward: the complete merging of Negro and white in a common society. There was no hesitation, no equivocation in the demanding of such a merger. In the party, Negro members were treated with more than equality, and white female party members went out of their way to demonstrate how serious Communists were in eliminating all social barriers between the two races. The slightest hesitation in social relations with Negro party members, and indeed, some felt, in sexual relations, made a member suspect, and might lead to denunciation. Social relations between Negroes and whites in the Communist Party were far more effective in permitting the party to reach Negroes than any higher policy hammered out by Moscow. The higher policy did mean that money and resources were available for Negro work, but the day-to-day work was based on the expression of concern for the immediate problems of Negroes, and, even more important, on a demonstration that the Communist Party was unique in its attitude to Negroes among the organizations in American life.

This is not to suggest that Communists had overcome the subtle and delicate problems surrounding the personal relations between Negroes and whites in America. Even when there is the best will on both sides, the wounds are too deep, the traumas too severe, the suspicions too close to the surface, the readiness to act in a special way when one detects the flag of race too great, for such relations often to rise to the level of simple social dealings. Negro-white relations are generally, even when both sides are relatively free of prejudice, too stiff or too hearty. Negroes were still suspicious of white Communists, and often enough had good grounds for the belief that they had not totally eradicated prejudice from their hearts. Despite all this, and despite the fact that the discovery of prejudice in Communist whites might be a greater shock than in non-Communist whites, the Communist party was unique—even in Right-Wing periods, when it did not stress Negro issues—in its effort to create mixed social situations.[6]

This uniqueness was shown, for example, in the trials of members for "white chauvinism." The most famous of these trials was that of August Yokinen, janitor for the Finnish Workers Club in Harlem, who had, it would appear, been impolite to Negroes who had come to a dance. What he had actually done hardly matters. On March 1, 1931, a huge mass meeting was held, in the form of a "trial." Yokinen pleaded his guilt, promised to reform, and was expelled. This was a model demonstration for many others, and the party believed these trials were important in helping it reach the Negro masses. But there came a time when there was too much of a good thing. "There has been a certain tendency for a large mass production of white chauvinism trials in which quality has been sacrificed to quantity . . ." asserted Browder in 1933. But where else in American life could one find any organization that considered it a crime for its members to be squeamish about mixed dancing? [7]

The show trial was only one of the techniques by which the party tried to show its special concern for Negroes. Along with the symbolic impact of the white-chauvinism trials was the perhaps more forceful impact of the nomination of a Negro for Vice-President in 1932. The Communist Party was always very short on electoral successes, and it would be hard to show that the scanty votes of William Z. Foster and James W. Ford in 1932 included many Negro votes (few Negroes could then vote). But despite the unimportance of elections in general in the Communist scheme of things, they did campaign for their tickets, they did issue literature—and there, for anyone to see, alongside a white man and running for the second highest post in the country, was a Negro.

Within the party, Negroes were rapidly pushed into positions of leadership. The party aimed at a high proportion of Negroes in convention delegations, and in leading committees, though it rarely could attain a high percentage with the forces available to it. By the 1934 convention of the party, it was able to muster thirty-nine Negro delegates in a convention of 233—but 25 per cent of these had joined within the previous nine months.[8]

On a humbler, but in the end more important, level, that of the party training schools, a serious effort was also made to get a high Negro representation. Of fifty-three students in full-time training schools in 1930-31, fully one quarter were Negro. Of forty-one students in 1932, twelve were Negro.[9] And on lower levels, too, Negroes were brought into the leadership; a sample of Unemployed Council leaders in Chicago in the 1930's showed twenty-one Negroes out of one hundred.[10]

Were Communists serious in their efforts to create Negro leaders? Did they push Negroes forward simply to have a Negro front behind which white leaders pulled the strings? Negro members often believed this. But the fact was that the Communist organizations always operated this way, with leaders behind the scenes acting with complete disdain for rank-and-file members and for those leaders beneath them in the hierarchy. Disdain and contempt were all but universal, and were felt by Communists in authority, white or colored, for all Communists and others not in authority, white or colored, without discrimination. Richard Wright speaks thus of his contact with a Negro Communist organizer: "His tone was more patronizing than that of a Southern white man." [11] Aside from the psychological residues of prejudice which even Communist training could not root out, the party was serious in its efforts to develop Negro leadership.

The Communists also had the great boon, in their efforts to recruit Negroes, of the Scottsboro Case. To manufacture white-chauvinism trials against Communists, whatever the party leaders' feeling that this had been helpful, was obviously less effective than having a real trial, dramatizing the oppression of the Southern Negro, and evoking a response from American Negroes greater than anything since the Civil War. The Communists "captured" the case—and a good case like this was of incalculable value. For the first time, Communists were able to enter Negro churches and other organizations. The sums that could be raised for such a case were enormous, and most of the money could go to the support of a staff of Communist organizers and fund-raisers. A whole periphery of organizations could be built around such a case, and many members brought into the party from them. The Communists were, therefore, always on the lookout for victims of injustice who might allow them to take over their "defense." [12]

In 1930, for the first time, a large number of Negroes entered the party. Stachel had said in 1929 that there were 150 to 200 Negroes in the party; a year later, Browder, referring to the same period, said there were then "hardly 50" Negroes in the party. This is where the party stood on the eve of the thirties. The big recruiting drive in 1930, which brought 6,167 new members into the party, also brought in the first big wave of Negro members—1,300. But the turnover of Negro members was particularly high, and it took a few years before the Negro membership rose above 1,000. In October 1931, there was a complaint that "particularly few Negroes have been brought into the Party," and it was reported that there were less than 1,000.[13]

Chicago was particularly effective in recruiting Negro members; New York lagged. In February 1932, 412 of 1,700 Chicago members were Negro; only 74 of 2,350 New York members.[14] In May 1935, it was reported that there were 2,227 Negro members in the party, exclusive of the Southern District,

which must have added a few more. This was 8 per cent of the
party membership at that time. It was simultaneously reported
that 792 of 5,300 recent recruits were Negroes, or 15 per cent.[15]
This was the pattern of Negro recruitment into the party for
many years. The party steadily recruited about twice as many
Negro members as the rolls showed at any time.

Thus, there were 2,649 Negro members in the party in January 1937, about 7 per cent of the total membership. In a big
recruiting drive of the following year, it was announced that
2,890 (17 per cent of all new recruits) were Negro, and that
the Negro membership of the party was 5,000. Yet four years
later, in 1942, the party still had only 3,200 Negro members,
about 7 per cent of the total membership, and this figure was
referred to as "really alarming." [16]

It is doubtful that the Negro membership ever rose much
above this percentage. In 1943 it was announced that 31 per
cent of 15,000 new recruits were Negro; in 1944 that 37 per
cent of 20,000 new recruits were Negro; and in 1946 that "one-
third" of 15,000 new recruits were Negro. Yet in these three
years the percentage of Negroes in the party as a whole was
given as 10, 14, and 14. And by 1946, the evidence suggests,
the party was inflating the figure of Negro membership. Fourteen per cent of the party in 1946 would have amounted to
7,000; in Foster's history it is asserted that 17 per cent of
the membership in 1947 and 1948, or 10,000, were Negroes!
Yet after 1945, when the party was reconstituted, there were
steady complaints that insufficient Negroes were being recruited; independent estimates are much lower; and the post-
1946 figures were probably simply inflated in an effort to make
the figures reflect the party's great political investment in the
effort to recruit Negroes.[17]

The figures demonstrate the serious problem of Negro fluctuation. It was a permanent problem, and it was plainly based on the fact that since the greatest efforts were being made to bring Negroes into the party, they entered with the lowest degree of indoctrination, with the least commitment, with the least knowledge, and consequently found it easiest to leave. As Max Steinberg pointed out in describing the efforts of the New York District to raise the proportion of Negroes and of industrial workers (it was low in both, and fluctuation was high in both categories), these "recruits come in to the Party as a result of . . . struggles our Party leads. . . . These workers, upon joining, have a limited understanding of what the Party is. . . ." [18] In the nature of the case, there was no way of solving this problem. Making it easy for Negroes to join meant taking in members of a lower level of knowledge, commitment, and motivation. In 1953, after years of the most intensive effort devoted to getting Negroes into the party, the same complaint and the same analysis is found: "Negro workers come into our Party primarily because of the Party's position on the Negro question and not the class struggle . . . but unless our Party comrades are imbued with a perspective of socialism and see in this the ultimate solution of the Negro question there is no basis for sustained Party membership." [19]

These quotations introduce another concern of the party in connection with its Negro membership: the difficulty of developing leadership and cadres from among this membership. Obviously, the same factors in Negro work that led to high fluctuation led to an over-all poor quality of the Negro membership, from the point of view of developing good Bolsheviks. The "Organization and Statistics" report of 1942 complained of this, and asserted that there were only three Negroes in leading posts in the party (Ford, Ray Hansborough, and Ben Davis). At this time, however, the party's emphasis on Negro rights was severely muted by its single-minded effort to show itself most loyal and consistent in support of the war. At a time when more Negroes than ever before in American history were moving north and west and into factories and shipyards, and were thus more easily accessible to party recruiting, the party played down any effort to demand equality for Negroes, and lost a great potential opportunity among them. This did not help it in its efforts to develop Negro leadership. In April 1945, John Williamson asserted that there was "very unsatisfactory promotion and training of Negro leaders. . . . We must abandon the practice of having white comrades in key posts of leadership in clubs in Negro communities, while Negro members are supposed to serve an 'apprenticeship.' " [20]

In the reconstituted party of 1945, during the first half-dozen years of the cold war, the Negro issue became one of the most important issues the party had. The treatment of Negroes in America not only was the one domestic issue it could develop freely, but it also served internationally to indict America before the world. The louder the party screamed that the Negroes were subject to "genocide" in the United States, the more this could be used as "evidence" by its friends abroad (and in the United Nations) that this was really so. And, as pointed out earlier, the more the party was forced into a position of near illegality by its support of cold-war (and hot-war) enemies, the more it felt that Negroes, the group with least reason to be patriotic, might be most responsive to party appeals. Yet even under these favorable circumstances, and despite huge efforts put forth in the form of leaflets, publications, organizers, it seemed difficult to develop a strong Negro cadre.

As said earlier, intensity in recruitment efforts inevitably meant members that were poor material for Bolshevization. But on the principle that there are no fortresses Bolsheviks cannot storm, that the weakness in the party's work was not "objective," but "subjective," the white membership was taken to task for being insufficiently bold in advancing Negro members. Part of the orgy of "self-criticism" that accompanied the expulsion of Browder emphasized his failings in developing Negro leadership. "We . . . indulged in sharp self-criticism for failure to develop . . . a strong corps of Negro Communist cadres . . . but we never gave practical organizational expression to the correct conclusions then drawn. . . . Many thousands . . . who entered our ranks failed to find the answers they sought, and thereupon produced the 'fluctuating Negro membership' problem which practically all districts report." [21]

The new and more "correct" policies, that is, the almost hysterical emphasis on Negroes, did little, it seems, to correct the problems of either fluctuating membership or weakness of Negro leadership. After the Smith Act, as mentioned previously, the party was to be regrouped in a structure of threes for security purposes. There would be a top three, each one of which was to be in touch with a trio below him, and so on, to seven levels, which would give (three to the seventh power) 3,150 in this structure in New York State. John Lautner, helping to set up this structure, reported: "When we checked the first four levels [that had been set up] we came to one conclusion, that we hit the bottom of the barrel too quick. . . . We came to another conclusion, that *no* Negro personnel were integrated into this structure in the top four levels in New York State. . . . We felt we were leaning backwards too much, in other words security too much at the expense of this over-all political question, the Negro question." [22]

The situation in New York was probably exceptional, for by the end of the forties and through the fifties, the party had a fairly large and reliable Negro cadre, at least enough to staff the national committees with a good number of Negro leaders. And this cadre, it would appear, also included some middle-level elements. In 1953, J. Edgar Hoover reported on a study of 5,395 leading members of the Communist Party: 411 were Negroes. This was less than the party would have liked, unquestionably, insufficient in number to merit the title of "party of the Negro people," but if almost 8 per cent of the leading members of the party were Negro, the vast labors that had gone into recruiting Negroes were not wasted.[23]

In the meantime, offsetting the gains in developing Negro leadership, the party had to reckon with the loss of large numbers of members in the white-chauvinism madness. Between 1949 and 1953, the party was engaged in a witch hunt to seek out anti-Negro members, and a large number were expelled for white chauvinism. Conceivably, among those expelled there were some who shared the general American prejudice against Negroes, but it is not likely that such people would have joined the Communist Party in the first place, and maintained membership after the powerful government and trade-union attacks beginning in 1949. Most of those expelled found themselves vilified for trivial failings. The party was less interested in actually rooting out white chauvinists than in demonstrating to Negroes the horror with which it viewed any hint of prejudice. But as in the case of other purges, it seemed hard to keep it in control, and the damage to the party soon outweighed any possible gain in influencing Negro opinion. (Indeed, some Negroes were also repelled by the spectacle, which inevitably focused attention on their race and emphasized their role as a "problem.")

The white-chauvinism charges hit the Jewish membership particularly strongly. Since Jews were largely middle class at this time, and living in middle-class communities and leading middle-class lives, there were many grounds for suspicion. Their communities might be all white; their apartment buildings all white; they went on vacations to Miami; they might even have Negro domestics. None of these was necessarily a proof of white chauvinism, but any reader of accounts of Communist interrogation techniques can see that from such a complex quite a good case could be made. In addition, the concentration on Negro issues heightened the characteristic insensitivity to issues affecting Jews. This contributed to a loss of Jewish fellow travelers that made itself felt as early as 1949.[24]

It is commonly said that the American Negroes resisted the appeal of Communism. If Communism's success among Negroes is measured by the organizations it influenced, the number of members it attracted, the newspapers that were sympathetic, the votes it obtained, its influence was indeed small. At the same time, because the party was unique in its attitude toward the Negro, there was perhaps less antipathy to the party generally among Negroes than elsewhere in American society. It is true that the party "used" the Negro issue—and this was perfectly clear to politically sophisticated Negroes. But at the same time, the party was the only institution in American life in which Negroes commonly worked with whites on a level of equality, which was truly color-blind, which was really indifferent to issues of race. The party "used" race politically but it did not take race seriously. The devoted party member did not react to race personally; if he did, it was a failing to be punished and removed. The party would lean over backward to obtain Negro members, to train them, to put them on delegations and perhaps in leadership positions. A Negro who knew the party could see the simple fact that if a Negro became a true Bolshevik, there was no limit to the position to which he might rise in the party; indeed, he might rise higher than a white of the same ability. If one thinks of the other organizations of American life—political parties, voluntary organizations, businesses—one becomes aware of how rare this simple workmanlike co-operation is between white and colored in American society. Organized labor is the only exception, and it is a partial exception.

There was another aspect of the Communist Party appeal to Negroes. Negroes have always demanded equality, but, as a matter of fact, equality is often not enough. After two hundred years of slavery, after a hundred years of freedom under conditions of poverty, poor education or none at all, and mistreatment, perhaps more than equality is necessary for the Negroes. And, in effect, the Communists demanded more than equality. Thus, in the United Automobile Workers, one of the most effective issues raised by the Communists was the attempt to elect a Negro to the top governing body.[25] This was, to be sure, a typically Communist tactic. Walter Reuther, president of the union, argued that men should be advanced on the grounds of merit, not race. This, he said, was the way the Communists worked; they put up Negroes for show. But as a matter of fact, if a Negro had been thus advanced, he might have become, quite independently of the origin of his advancement, an effective leader.

From the point of view of American Negroes, there was little to object to in this Communist policy. After the war, the Communist Party made a strong effort to get the normal seniority clauses of union contracts suspended for Negroes. Last to be hired in the labor shortage, they would be the first, according to regular union procedures, to be fired.[26] Again, the appeal was made to Negro workers in the unions not to allow this special demand for Negro workers to affect the operation of a basic union principle. But general principles that mean justice are often suspended to correct special cases of injustice, as when the immigration laws are suspended to let in a body of political refugees, or tax moneys are made available to those suffering from flood or other disasters. Negroes are the victims of a man-made disaster more serious than any flood, and if the coming of the war had meant the fortuitous entry of many Negroes into industry, it could reasonably have been argued—and not by Communists alone—that some special provision might be adopted to help a larger number hold on to those jobs. In other words, while the Communist policies for Negroes were adopted to attract Negroes to the Communist Party, and while they were fought on grounds of general principle by the opponents of the Communists, they were also the kinds of issues that would legitimately attract Negroes, and they did. (Many Negroes of course resisted the "special treatment" that Communists insisted upon.)

The Communists also could draw upon another source of sympathy for Communism among Negroes: Soviet Russian policy on minorities, and the Russian people's personal liking for Negroes. Negroes who visited the Soviet Union found an even more favorable response to them than in France. This kind of personal contact affected very few Negroes directly. But Negroes could read in the writings of Langston Hughes and Claude McKay and Paul Robeson how different the Soviet Union was in its race attitudes from the United States. This, too, contributed to a positive image of Communists and Communism among American Negroes.

But however positive the image of Communism for American Negroes, it could not become a mass movement and a mass enthusiasm among them, for, after all, what could the Communists do for the Negroes?

To be a Communist in addition to being a Negro was to compound difficulties. From the Negro point of view, it was fine, if peculiar, that the Communists accepted Negroes as social equals.

It was fine that they took positions that were good for the Negroes. But this tiny and disreputable sect did not generally have
the power to be really helpful to Negroes. Indeed, many Negroes
feared that Communist support for certain policies would con-
tribute to their being labeled "Communist," and would mean
less support for them from white Americans. Yet to say that
the Communists failed among the Negroes slights a rather complex situation. They failed—but, to repeat, they created a unique
image among Negroes, and it is certain that Negroes never
viewed the party with the same kind of strong hostility that was
common for Americans in general.[27]

There are other reasons for the limitation of Communist influences among Negroes besides the fact that Communists could
not do much for Negroes, except make things more difficult for
them. There is, first, the fact that there was no large pool of
Socialists or former Socialists, or, indeed, ideological radicals of
any kind, among Negroes. There had been hardly any in the
Socialist Party; its growth preceded the period of heaviest Negro
immigration to the North, and, in any case, it refused to take
any stand on the questions that affected Negroes.[28] The racial
hostility of American workingmen and their organizations also
restricted any sympathy Negroes might have had for the Left,
which so enthusiastically championed organized labor. There
was thus no important ideological base among the Negroes that
favored the Communist Party.

American Negroes have a rich and varied organizational life,[29]
but these organizations are primarily social, on the one hand,
and religious, on the other. Neither kind offers a good target
for Communist infiltration. The Negro community is relatively
weak in the kind of public-minded, secular, voluntary organizations that Communists might have successfully penetrated. A
number of Negro ministers became fellow travelers and even

party members, almost entirely on the basis of the pro-Negro policies of the party, but it was quite out of the question for the Negro church to become a base of Communist influence in Negro communities.[30]

There was, therefore, no good organizational base for the party to work in. There did exist the National Urban League and the National Association for the Advancement of Colored People, and the Communists were untiring in their efforts to penetrate these organizations, which supplied almost the only organizational channel into the Negro community they could use. But these organizations had sophisticated anti-Communist leaders, and could see no advantage in letting the Communists get in.[31] Thus, without support from either a sympathetic pre-existing ideology or susceptible organizational structures, the Communists, despite their great efforts, were limited in their ability to gain Negro members and cadres and to penetrate the Negro community.

CONCLUSION

This study has been both a history and an analysis. It is time to pull together the analytic themes that have again and again been called upon to explain the pattern of response to Communism in America. As we have seen, the party had a theory that explained where it might find support. Sustained in part by the theory were the shifting policies of the party which, at different times, focused the efforts to get members on different sections of the social body. Theory and policies were not, in general, fulfilled in American reality. The party found it difficult to get native-born workers as members, though it eventually developed a sizable membership of trade-union activists. It found in the years of the Depression a surprising response in professional and middle-class groups, among whom it had at first made no special effort to find members, and it found a surprising response among Jews. Yet its intense efforts to recruit Negroes and develop Negro leadership were only poorly rewarded by results.

What explains this pattern of success and failure in the different segments of American society? The common understanding of Communism sees it as the response of the poor and the oppressed and the exploited to the circumstances of their lives, and this was the party's own way of understanding the matter, too. The most oppressed, the most exploited, the most unfortunate, it believed, would respond to its appeals. This meant the factory workers, the poorest farmers and share-croppers, the Negroes.

This is not the way things turned out, and yet there is a good deal of truth in the common understanding. As pointed out in Chapter II, where the various ethnic working-class groups were discussed, there seemed to be no precise relationship between their general economic and social position and their response to the party. But there was a general relationship. The earlier and more-assimilated ethnic groups did not enter the party—though it is hard to know whether there were so few Irish because they were an earlier ethnic group or because they were Catholic. The later groups, with important exceptions, such as the Poles—also strongly Catholic—seemed to show a greater tendency to come into the party. Economic and social circumstances did set a general frame, in which elements of religion and culture operated to make a complex picture of response.

Similarly, while there was never a large movement of the factory working class into the party, it was during the Depression that the scene was laid for inroads among them. During the Depression, too, there was considerable response from the unemployed. And in time, a part of the factory working class did join the party. It was during the Depression that the party grew large and developed some importance. There was no simple direct relationship between the misery of recruits and their response to the party. But their general conditions, again, did set a frame in which other factors operated. Here the important additional factors were the rise of the labor movement, the Communist organizational role within it, and the party's consequent capacity to recruit members.

The greatest disparity between economic and social circumstances and party response was found among the Jews, the middle class, and the Negroes. The Jews should not have joined the party, the Negroes should have—if this general theory of response on the basis of misery is to be considered proved. To save this theory, it can, of course, be argued that, despite the relatively good economic position of Jews, their rapid rise to middle-class status produced certain strains—a sense of discrimination, a feeling of oppression and exploitation, if not its reality. If the "reference group" [1] of Jews was the established middle class, then they might well have had such feelings. If their "reference group" was the social situation from which they had just risen, and to which they were closely enough related through parents, relatives, friends, memory, they would feel quite satisfied. Perhaps it can be argued that deprivation was always involved in party membership; yet the notion of deprivation has to be stretched a good deal to defend this theory, and even then it leaves too much unexplained.

And yet the common understanding that Communism is a response to deprivation, exploitation, and misery has a good deal of truth in it. It was, after all, in the Depression that the party grew, that its influence expanded to all sections of the country, that it was able to find some response in even such an unlikely group as the farmers, that it found that Americans of all sorts and of no particular radical background showed up at party headquarters and became Communists. This general frame of social and economic conditions is sound enough as an explanation of Communist success and failure, but must be supplemented by two other explanatory themes: the role of ideology and the role of organization.

Catholicism often acted as an independent force to inhibit entrance into the party. But other ideologies served to facilitate entry into the party. Radical ideologies, particularly when they were institutionalized in a group through established organizations, and when they had become familiar to a group because of its history, served as an important basis for successful Communist activity, independently of the economic circumstances of the group. Ideology played a role in leading certain ethnic groups into the party. The relative weakness of ideology among trade-union members made them less accessible to the party and weakened their attachment to it. Ideology played a role in Jewish middle-class groups in opening them to the appeal of the party and leading them to a stronger commitment. The absence of ideology among Negroes contributed to a weak Negro response to party appeals.

By "ideology" I mean primarily the tendency in a group to see the world in traditional Socialist terms. This ideology is widespread among the working classes and intellectuals of Europe. For various historical reasons, it is not widespread in America. While it achieved some partial hold among American intellectuals, its greatest spread was in certain immigrant groups who had learned the Socialist interpretation of historical events in Europe. And it is because of this localization of Socialist ideology in America that our analysis has again and again been forced to work in terms of given ethnic groups rather than of other social categories.

But was Socialist ideology then a kind of injection, given once and for all at a certain time? Could it not be learned anew and afresh in America as an outcome of the social circumstances of a social group and the spread of propaganda among it? In America, Socialism, and Socialist ideology, was more an import than a locally produced product. There was a certain amount of native Socialism in this country, but the imported variety was more important. There are certain generations which undergo a great change in outlook. Socialism in Europe marked whole generations. The immigrant Jewish workers who came to this country before World War I and the immigrant Finnish workers who came at the same time were such genera-tions.² The change from a religious to a Socialist and secular outlook that characterized these groups was a revolution in thinking and perceiving of such dimensions that it cast its influ-ence on succeeding generations. True, it required a depression and other social developments for this influence to make itself felt in action. Yet it was there to be aroused under certain con-ditions.

In America, a major Socialist revolution in the way large numbers of people view events never occurred. Before World War I, it seemed as if America were about to create its own Socialist world, but this was never of the dimensions that were characteristic of Europe.³ Nor was the generation of the Depres-sion turned into Socialists; they were turned into Democrats, New Dealers, supporters of the Welfare State. The peculiar vision of Socialism, which has played such an enormous role in world history, and still seems to play such a role in Asia, Africa, and Latin America, did not seize Americans. In the absence in America of the general seedbed of Socialist perception in which Communists operate everywhere, the more localized pools of such ideology were utilized, and these were to be found among certain ethnic groups, and among intellectual groups.

If ideology has been one major guiding line in helping to interpret the pattern of response to Communist appeals, a second, and equally important, one has been organization. This theme has emerged in a number of places. In Chapter I, I pointed out that Socialism was strongest and most persistent in those parts of the population where it was connected with strong organizations (such as the Jewish trade unions). In Chapters II, IV, and V, I pointed to the different organizational patterns (independent of any political attitudes) that characterize different groups, and the degree to which these organizations supply openings for Communist work either simply by existing, and so creating channels, or by having a certain political or social orientation that makes it possible for Communists to work within them. In Chapter III, I discussed the varying organizational patterns in existence in one area of Communist strength (the trade-union movement), and how these made it possible either for Communists to maintain control or for their enemies to eject them. And throughout, we have seen evidences of the organizational mania of the Communists—their absolute conviction that the correct organizational approach, the correct form, would give power and influence.

One need not go this far, but to understand the pattern of Communist success in different ethnic groups, among Negroes, in the labor movement, in middle-class groups, one is again and again drawn to the question of organization: How are they organized, if at all? What channels do they open to a group like the Communists? Do they permit the members to remove the leaders? Do they give the leaders important influence over mechanisms of control and means of propaganda? The whole line of investigation developed by Philip Selznick, S. M. Lipset, and others,[4] is most important for the general understanding of Communist influence and power.

The two interpretative themes suggested by the terms "ideology" and "organization" help one to understand the varying responses in the American population to Communist efforts. Over-all, the response was weak, weaker than in any other great industrial power, weaker than in any other great country, industrial or agricultural. Communists operated in every social sphere, in every region, among every group. Here and there, one can point to a partial success, or a failure less absolute and complete than was general in this country. Between 1938 and 1948, Communists wielded important influence over a section of the labor movement and liberal opinion. But over-all, Communism in America was a failure.

Here the Communists worked in an unfruitful field. Martin Diamond has summed up the reasons Socialism failed in America; they are also the reasons Communism failed, for they are what is most fundamental about America:

> What caused the American workers to act unlike the European workers who turned to socialism? In Europe, what the workers wanted had to be fought for as class against other classes, against the regime. Great want and the necessity for bitter class struggle made them vulnerable to the millennial dream for which socialists supplied the inspiration and the leadership. Whatever it was the American workers wanted, it could be sought with the hope of success by individuals against other individuals or nature, within the existing order. What accounts for this? The massive if simple answer lies in America's democracy and wealth. Democracy because it habituated men to the orderly . . . pursuit of goals. Wealth because America's bounty and dynamic economy made possible an astonishingly high level of satisfaction for the wants encouraged by the democracy and pursued by democratic means. It is America's two most distinctive features, each and together, which account for the unique non-socialist bent of the American worker.[5]

In America even the most oppressed and the most miserable could see that the normal processes of American democracy, operating in this huge and wealthy land, could give them more than the Communists ever could. Self-interest, which according to the Communists' own theory should be the spur that brings the masses to them, operated here to drive them away. And so the Communists had to resort, whether they knew it or not, to the special quirks of history that made some groups, at some times, open to them; they operated in these openings with their mixture of organizational skill and moral blindness, and achieved some successes. But in the end, these strains and twists in American democracy were insufficient to give them lasting success.

ACKNOWLEDGMENTS · NOTES · INDEX

ACKNOWLEDGMENTS

Clinton Rossiter has been the patient and helpful general editor of the entire series of which this book is a part; and he has given this volume a meticulous critical reading which made it possible for me to improve it greatly, in substance and in style. Theodore Draper, Daniel Bell, Bernard Barber, S. M. Lipset, and Melech Epstein also read the book and made helpful suggestions and corrections; and Doxey Wilkerson gave particular attention to Chapter V, and helped me to improve that. I am indebted to Frank Meyer and Max Silver for particularly enlightening interviews, and to Nancy Edelman for her competent aid in cleaning up a mass of messy footnotes. I have indicated in the footnotes of this book my indebtedness to all those who have written on the Communist movement, of their own experience and the experience of others, and to those who have placed their story, voluntarily or involuntarily, on the public record.

NOTES

INTRODUCTION

INTRODUCTION

1. Did the American Communist Party differ from other Communist parties in the kind of membership it had? Is this point of view as to the significance of membership relevant for a study of the American party? I do not believe that the differences between the American and other parties were such as to make a study of membership less important for the American party. While there have been important changes in the world Communist movement in recent years which raise serious questions as to whether the organizational uniformity of the Communist parties will be maintained in the future, such uniformity was almost universal for the period with which this book deals, the years from 1920 to 1950. Communists everywhere read the same theoretical and organizational texts, used the same slogans, very often used the same language, which must presumably have been as clumsy in other tongues as it was in English. The American party was, of course, different in many ways from other parties, but these differences arose from the nature of American society and the composition of the American population, not from any major differences in the attitudes of the leadership of the party as to what was important, and how it was to be achieved.

It is futile to attempt to document any such central conception of the Communist Party as that here presented. It arises from many years of study of the literature of the Communist movement, much discussion with students of the Communist movement and with former Communists, much reading of the huge literature, scholarly and popular, on Communism. Two books, however, express for me as well as any I know this organizational aspect of Communism: Philip Selznick's *The Organizational Weapon: A Study of Bolshevik Strategy and Tactics* (New York: McGraw-Hill, 1952), and Frank B. Meyer's *The Moulding of Communists* (New York: Harcourt, Brace, 1961).

2. Gabriel Almond, *et al., The Appeals of Communism* (Princeton: Princeton University Press, 1954). See, too, the unpublished thesis of Herbert Krugman, "The Interplay of Social and Psychological Factors in Political Deviance: An Inquiry into Some Factors Underlying the Motivation of Intellectuals Who Became Communists" (Columbia University, 1952), and Morris Ernst and David Loth, *Report on the American Communist* (New York: Holt, 1952).

3. Among the volumes to be published in the "Communism in American Life" series will be works dealing with writers (by Daniel Aaron), artists (by Donald Drew Egbert), and the mass media (by Moshe Decter).

CHAPTER ONE · THE BACKGROUND OF COMMUNIST PARTY MEMBERSHIP

1. Alexander Trachtenberg, ed., *The American Labor Year Book, 1917-1918* (New York: The Rand School of Social Science, 1918), p. 340.
2. Ira Kipnis, *The American Socialist Movement 1897-1912* (New York: Columbia University Press, 1952), pp. 19-20.
3. *Ibid.,* p. 104; David A. Shannon, *The Socialist Party of America: A History* (New York: Macmillan, 1955), p. 94.
4. This attempt to characterize the Socialist Party on the eve of World War I is based on such standard histories as those of Daniel Bell ("The Background and Development of Marxian Socialism in the United States," in *Socialism and American Life,* ed. by Donald Drew Egbert and Stow Persons, Princeton: Princeton University Press, 1952, Vol. I, pp. 267-328); Shannon (*op. cit.,* pp. 43-125); and Kipnis (*op. cit.,* pp. 199-429), as well as on data referred to in these notes. The only statistics

I know of on the proportions of foreign-born and native-born in the Socialist Party are for 1908, when the party had 40,000 members. These statistics show that 71 per cent of the members had been born in the United States, 8.5 per cent in Germany, 5 per cent in Denmark, 2 per cent in Finland, 9.5 per cent elsewhere: Nathan Fine, *Labor and Farmer Parties in the United States 1828-1928* (New York: the Rand School of Social Science, 1926), p. 324. The picture given here of the party as of 1914 differs in placing much more weight on the immigrant sector. However, the party had from 1908 to 1912 tripled in membership, then undergone a decline of some 20,000. In addition, from 1908 to 1914, the part of the party known to be foreign-born, those in the foreign-language federations, had increased greatly. It would, of course, be helpful if there were figures broken down by birthplace for other years; and equally helpful if there were figures for occupations of members, but there are not.

5. *The American Labor Year Book, 1916* (New York: The Rand School of Social Science, 1916), pp. 95-96.

6. *Ibid.,* p. 99.

7. Oscar Ameringer, *If You Don't Weaken* (New York: Holt, 1940), pp. 227-235, 256-275, 283-287, 305-314, 347-364.

8. For the background of the politics of Great Plains farmers, see S. M. Lipset, *Agrarian Socialism* (Berkeley, California: University of California Press, 1950).

9. Vernon H. Jensen, *Heritage of Conflict* (Ithaca, New York: Cornell University Press, 1950), p. 4.

10. S. M. Lipset, *Political Man* (New York: Doubleday, 1960), pp. 112, 194, 231, 234, 375.

11. Bill Haywood, *Bill Haywood's Book* (New York: International, 1922), pp. 23, 31, 71.

12. Ella Reeve Bloor, *We Are Many* (New York: International, 1940), pp. 39-81.

13. Kipnis, *op. cit.,* p. 270.

14. *Ibid.,* p. 247.

15. Bloor, *op. cit.,* p. 80.

16. Kipnis, *op. cit.,* p. 397.

17. "Probably more immigrant socialists were lost to the cause in the United States than were won from the ranks of the newcomers." Marcus Hansen, *The Immigrant in American History*

(Cambridge, Massachusetts: Harvard University Press, 1948), p. 95.

18. For example: Max D. Danish, *The World of David Dubinsky* (Cleveland: World Publishing Company, 1957), pp. 13-20; Matthew Josephson, *Sidney Hillman: Statesman of American Labor* (Garden City, New York: Doubleday, 1952), pp. 26-35.

19. John Kolehmainen, *Sow the Golden Seed* (Fitchburg, Massachusetts: Raivajaa Publishing Company, 1955), p. 26.

20. John Kolehmainen, "The Inimitable Marxists: The Finnish Immigrant Socialists," *Michigan History*, XXXVI (1952), p. 399.

21. Kolehmainen, *Sow the Golden Seed*, pp. 16-17.

22. Shannon, *op. cit.*, p. 44; Kipnis, *op. cit.*, pp. 272-274.

23. Shannon, *op. cit.*, p. 44.

24. Kolehmainen, "The Inimitable Marxists," *loc. cit.*, p. 397; Trachtenberg, *op. cit.*, p. 349.

25. Shannon, *op. cit.*, p. 45.

26. Kipnis, *op. cit.*, pp. 275-276.

27. John R. Commons, David J. Saposs, Helen L. Sumner, E. B. Mittleman, H. E. Hoagland, John B. Andrews, Selig Perlman, *History of Labor in the United States, 1896-1932* (New York: Macmillan, 1935), Vol. III, p. 41.

28. Trachtenberg, *op. cit.*, p. 366.

29. For the story of Haywood's recall, see Kipnis, *op. cit.*, Chap. 15. For the vote on the recall, see Shannon, *op. cit.*, pp. 77-78.

30. Kolehmainen, "The Inimitable Marxists," *loc. cit.*, pp. 400-401.

31. Paul F. Brissenden, *The I.W.W.: A Study of American Syndicalism* (New York: Columbia University Press, 1919), pp. 333, 339.

32. Ralph Chaplin, *Wobbly: The Rough-and-Tumble Story of an American Radical* (Chicago: University of Chicago Press, 1948), p. 201.

33. David J. Saposs, *Left-Wing Unionism* (New York: International, 1926), p. 145.

34. Theodore Draper, *The Roots of American Communism* (New York: Viking, 1957), p. 150.

35. A masterly account of the issues and strains that created the Left in the American Socialist Party is given in Draper, *op. cit.*, pp. 17-184.

36. Joseph Rappaport, "Jewish Immigrants and World War I: A

Study of American Yiddish Press Reactions" (unpublished doctoral dissertation, Columbia University, 1951), pp. 75-76, 200.

37. *Ibid.*, pp. 268, 273, 282.
38. *Ibid.*, pp. 316-317, 321.
39. Trachtenberg, *op. cit.*, p. 341.
40. Rappaport, *op. cit.*, pp. 285, 287-288.
41. Shannon, *op. cit.*, p. 104.
42. *Ibid.*, p. 128.
43. Draper, *op. cit.*, p. 138.
44. James Oneal, *American Communism* (New York: The Rand Book Store, 1927), p. 53.
45. *Ibid.*
46. Draper, *op. cit.*, pp. 66-69.
47. Oneal, *op. cit.*, p. 53. Conceivably, the entire Lettish group, or the entire potential membership for a pro-Bolshevik organization, had *already* been mobilized by December 1918. This is a reasonable explanation, particularly in the light of the fact that the Lettish group in the United States was tiny. In 1930, there were only 8,000 foreign-born Lettish speakers in the United States.

CHAPTER TWO · FOREIGN-BORN WORKERS AND THE PARTY IN THE TWENTIES

1. Theodore Draper, *The Roots of American Communism* (New York: Viking, 1957), pp. 114, 191, 392; Irving Howe and Lewis Coser, *The American Communist Party, a Critical History: 1919-1957* (Boston: Beacon, 1957), p. 95 n.
2. Draper, *op. cit.*, p. 158.
3. David A. Shannon, *The Socialist Party of America: A History* (New York: Macmillan, 1955), p. 163.
4. Workers (Communist) Party of America, *The 4th National Convention* (Chicago: Daily Worker Publishing Co., 1925), pp. 27-37.
5. Jack Stachel, "Organization Report to the Sixth Convention of the Communist Party of the U.S.A.," *The Communist,* April 1929, pp. 180-181.

6. Calculated from figures in *The 4th National Convention,* pp. 27, 29, 33, 39.

7. The early constitutions of the Communist Party specifically provide for the translation of all statements by the Central Executive Committee. The constitutions are reprinted in Committee on Un-American Activities, U.S. House of Representatives, *Organized Communism in the United States,* House Report No. 625, 83rd Congress, 2nd Session, August 19, 1953, pp. 64-65, 75.

8. Draper, *op. cit.,* p. 158.

9. Adolph Germer, "Minutes of the Party National Executive Committee Meeting in Chicago, May 24-30," *The Bulletin,* issued June 19, 1919, by National Office, Socialist Party. In the first six months of 1918, the average membership of the Polish Federation was 817. "Report of the Executive Secretary to the National Executive Committee (of the Socialist Party)," August 8, 1918, p. 10. In 1918, the Hungarian Federation had a membership of 1,037. Alexander Trachtenberg, ed., *The American Labor Year Book, 1917-1918* (New York: The Rand School of Social Science, 1918), p. 340.

10. Draper, *op. cit.,* p. 188.

11. *Ibid.,* p. 427, n 21.

12. *Ibid.,* pp. 332-333.

13. In *The 4th National Convention,* pp. 43-51, there are reports from only fifteen foreign-language groups. However, the detailed membership figures for the years 1922-25, on pp. 27-37, give eighteen foreign-language groups. The matter is not simple, however, for the membership figures omit the Bulgarian group, on which a full report is to be found in the proceedings, and include a Slovenian group, for which a small membership figure is given for one year. The Slovenian group is nowhere else referred to.

14. *The 2nd Congress of the Communist International as Reported and Interpreted by the Official Newspapers of Soviet Russia* (Washington: Government Printing Office, 1920), p. 154.

15. *The Communist,* August 15, 1920, pp. 5-11; reprinted in Committee on Un-American Activities, U.S. House of Representatives, *The Communist Conspiracy: Strategy and Tactics of World Communism; Part I, Communism Outside the United States, Section E, The Comintern and the CPUSA,* House Re-

port No. 2244, 84th Congress, 2nd Session, May 29, 1956, pp. 28, 30-31.

16. Draper, *op. cit.,* pp. 386, 456, n 26.

17. Draper, *op. cit.,* p. 279.

18. *The Worker,* August 25, 1923, p. 1; as quoted in Committee on Un-American Activities, *The Communist Conspiracy . . . Part I . . . Section E,* pp. 190-191.

19. *The Second Year of the Workers Party of America: Report of the Central Executive Committee to the Third National Convention Held in Chicago, Illinois, Dec. 30, 31, 1923, and Jan. 1, 2, 1924,* reprinted in Special Committee on Un-American Activities, U.S. House of Representatives, *Investigation of Un-American Propaganda Activities in the United States, Part I, Appendix,* 76th Congress, 1st Session, 1940, p. 386.

20. *International Press Correspondence,* February 7, 1924, p. 58, as quoted in Committee on Un-American Activities, *Organized Communism . . . ,* p. 192.

21. The best and clearest discussion of Bolshevization is in Theodore Draper, *American Communism and Soviet Russia* (New York: Viking, 1960), Chap. 7.

22. *Bolshevising the Communist International, Report of the Enlarged Executive of the Communist International, March 21st to April 14th, 1925* (London: Communist Party of Great Britain, 1925), p. 163.

23. *Ibid.,* p. 162.

24. *Ibid.,* pp. 45-46.

25. This same phrase ("a small party in a big industrial country") occurs in a different context in the proceedings of the Comintern in 1925. Appended to the important passage (quoted earlier) which asserts that "the principal . . . organizational form of every Bolshevik Party is the factory Party nucleus . . ." there is a footnote which reads: "There are cases where such reorganization [on a factory and workshop basis] should not be forced, for example: small parties in big industrial countries." *Ibid.,* p. 163. In view of the fact that the American party qualified perfectly for this exemption, and that nevertheless the reorganization of the American party was carried through almost immediately, one wonders just what the point of this footnote was, and whether there is any significance to

Cannon's use of the same formulation to press for reorganization.

26. *Ibid.,* pp. 45-46.
27. Committee on Un-American Activities, *Organized Communism* . . . , pp. 86-87.
28. Draper, *American Communism and Soviet Russia,* p. 187.
29. *Ibid.,* pp. 187-188.
30. Charles Ruthenberg, "From the Third Through the Fourth Convention of the Workers (Communist) Party," *Workers Monthly,* October 1925, pp. 533-536.
31. Martin Abern, "The Work of the Organization Conference," *Workers Monthly,* April 1926, p. 279.
32. Stachel, *op. cit.,* p. 181.
33. Computed from figures in *The 4th National Convention,* pp. 27-38.
34. *The Communist International Between the Fifth and the Sixth World Congresses, 1924-8* (London: Communist Party of Great Britain, 1928), p. 350.
35. Minutes of the Political Committee, January 14, 1927.
36. *Party Organizer,* February 1930, p. 10.
37. *Ibid.,* July-August 1928, p. 12.
38. Stenographic typescript of Organization Conference, C.P.U.S.A., March 21, 1930, p. 151.
39. *Party Organizer,* February 1930, p. 10.
40. Resolution of the Presidium of the E.C.C.I., July 1, 1927, quoted in *The Communist International Between the Fifth and the Sixth World Congresses,* p. 336.
41. "Open Letter of the E.C.C.I. to the Convention of the Workers (Communist) Party of America," *Inprecorr,* March 1, 1929, reprinted in Committee on Un-American Activities, *The Communist Conspiracy . . . Part I . . . Section E,* p. 55.
42. Stachel, *op. cit.,* p. 241.
43. *Ibid.,* p. 185.
44. Ossip Piatnitsky, *The Organization of a World Party* (London: Communist Party of Great Britain, 1928), p. 37.
45. *Party Organizer,* July-August 1928, p. 15.
46. *Ibid.,* February 1930, p. 9.
47. Organization Conference, March 21, 1930, pp. 151-60 (so numbered in original).
48. *Party Organizer,* July-August 1928, p. 15.

49. J. Mogul, in *ibid.,* June 1931, p. 5.
50. Organization Conference, March 21, 1930, pp. 151-60, 260, 337, 376-377.
51. Draper, *The Roots of American Communism,* pp. 159, 181, 188.
52. Draper, *American Communism and Soviet Russia,* pp. 89, 191.
53. Special Committee on Un-American Activities, *Investigation of Un-American Propaganda Activities . . . Part I, Appendix,* p. 353.
54. Committee on Un-American Activities, *The Communist Conspiracy . . . Part I . . . Section E,* p. 79.
55. Special Committee on Un-American Activities, *Investigation of Un-American Propaganda Activities . . . Part I, Appendix,* p. 353.
56. *The 4th National Convention,* p. 145.
57. Minutes of the Political Committee.
58. Organization Conference, March 21, 1930, pp. 121-125, 151-160.
59. *Ibid.,* p. 193.
60. *Ibid.,* pp. 121-125.
61. *Ibid.,* pp. 1271-1275.
62. The best account of this incident is in Howe and Coser, *op. cit.,* pp. 209-211.
63. Organization Conference, March 21, 1930, pp. 117-120.
64. *Ibid.,* p. 128.
65. *Ibid.,* p. 183.
66. Benjamin Gitlow, *I Confess* (New York: Dutton, 1940), p. 470.
67. Special Committee on Un-American Activities, *Investigation of Un-American Propaganda Activities . . . Part I, Appendix,* pp. 346-347.
68. Minutes of the Political Committee, October 13, 1926.
69. Organization Conference, March 21, 1930, p. 1196.
70. James Cannon, *The Struggle for a Proletarian Party* (New York: Pioneer, 1943), p. 24, as quoted in Draper, *American Communism and Soviet Russia,* p. 199.
71. Gitlow, *op. cit.,* p. 228.
72. Personal interview, August 14, 1956.
73. *Brownell* v. *Communist Party of the United States,* Subversive Activities Control Board Hearings, 1952, pp. 9166-9177.
74. As quoted in Draper, *American Communism and Soviet Russia,* pp. 183-184.
75. Draper, *The Roots of American Communism,* p. 393.

76. *The 4th National Convention,* pp. 40-41; Stachel, *op. cit.,* p. 182.
77. William Z. Foster, *History of the Communist Party of the United States* (New York: International, 1952), p. 205.
78. David M. Schneider, *The Workers' (Communist) Party and American Trade Unions* (Baltimore: The Johns Hopkins Press, 1928), p. 28.
79. Foster, *op. cit.,* p. 231.
80. Stachel, *op. cit.,* p. 186.
81. *Brownell* v. *Communist Party,* pp. 9156-9650.
82. Yaroslav Y. Chyz in 1948 drew up a list of every foreign-language group in which there was any trace of Communist organization or in which or for which Communist periodicals were published—"Communist and Pro-Soviet Press and Periodicals among the Nationality Groups in the U.S.A.," March, 1948. I am deeply indebted to Mr. Chyz for his permission to study and refer to this unpublished document.
83. *The 4th National Convention,* p. 42.
84. See Special Committee to Investigate Communist Activities in the United States, U.S. House of Representatives, *Investigation of Communist Propaganda,* Report No. 2290, 71st Congress, 3rd Session, January 17, 1931, p. 20.
85. See Marcus Lee Hansen, *The Immigrant in American History* (Cambridge, Massachusetts: Harvard University Press, 1948), Chap. IV; Oscar Handlin, *The Uprooted* (Boston: Little, Brown, 1951), pp. 217-218. This question of the conservatism of immigrants cannot be considered settled by the general views of the greatest of American historians of immigration. Hansen is conceivably influenced by his concentration on earlier immigrant groups (Scandinavian, German, Irish), who did show, in varying degrees, this conservatism, and reflected strong church influences. Some of these groups (as against later ones) became farmers, and this certainly also influenced their political development. Among the later immigrant groups, there were many in which radical influences, and, in particular, Communist influences, were strong.
86. Melech Epstein, who was one of the founders of the *Freiheit,* editor in chief in the late twenties, and associated with the newspaper in various capacities during the thirties, writes: "The *Freiheit* at the peak of the struggle [in the late twenties] never went beyond a paid circulation of 14,000 throughout the

country, including 1,800 in Canada. . . . (The *Freiheit* began without an A.B.C. check, and the management, wishing to hide the deeply disappointing circulation, greatly inflated it in the first post office report. As the paper had to show a steady growth, the subsequent reports could but tell of a proportionate climb in the number of readers. . . .)" *The Jew and Communism, 1919-1941* (New York: Trade Union Sponsoring Committee, 1959), p. 138. As for the degree of the inflation: for 1930, Ayer's *Directory of Newspapers and Periodicals* reported a "sworn" circulation of 64,500; in 1935, a circulation of 47,564. In 1940, Ayer's reported 51,246 (Post Office Statement). In 1947, the circulation of the *Freiheit* was reported to the Post Office as 20,911. Melech Epstein's statement refers to the earlier period. Max Silver, who was on the staff of the *Freiheit* in Philadelphia and Los Angeles in the thirties, and active in important positions in the Communist Party in Los Angeles in the forties, estimated *Freiheit* circulation at its peak to be 15,000 to 20,000, which would correspond to the figures being reported from the later 1940's on. This information for the *Freiheit* suggests that the percentage of Yiddish newspaper circulation that was Communist in 1930 was only 4 per cent, instead of the 12 per cent given in Table II. (The other major Yiddish newspapers reported A.B.C. figures.) There is no comparable evidence on the basis of which other figures may be adjusted, for, as pointed out in the text, there are no A.B.C. figures for the non-Jewish newspapers, and, conceivably, in all groups inflation may have been high. It is also possible that the reasons for the inflation by the *Freiheit* did not exist in the other groups.

87. In the Chyz report, *op. cit.*, there was only one publication for the Latvian group, and that was Communist. The only large ethnic group for which a comparable situation prevailed was the Croatian, in which during the late forties there was only one daily, a Communist one. Committee on Un-American Activities, U.S. House of Representatives, *Report on the American Slav Congress and Associated Organizations*, House Report No. 1951, 81st Congress, 2nd Session, June 26, 1949, p. 52.

CHAPTER THREE · NATIVE WORKERS AND TRADE-UNION INFLU-
ENCE AND THE PARTY

1. These assertions, and other general comments on the party,
   have been based on these standard sources: the two volumes by
   Theodore Draper—*The Roots of American Communism* (New
   York: Viking, 1957), and *American Communism and Soviet
   Russia* (New York: Viking, 1960); and Irving Howe and
   Lewis Coser, *The American Communist Party, a Critical History: 1919-1957* (Boston: Beacon, 1957).
2. *Party Organizer*, May-June 1934, p. 13; "The Party Position
   on Shop Papers," *Party Builder*, April 1929, p. 4.
3. This table is intended to give the broad picture of the growth
   and decline of the party from the beginning of the thirties to
   the middle of the fifties. The membership of the party can vary
   depending on whether one takes dues-paying members, registered members, or some estimate built up by adding members
   recruited since registration to the registered members. The
   dues-paying membership is generally the smallest figure. Earl
   Browder asserted in 1934 that dues payments averaged 90 per
   cent of the membership. *Party Organizer*, May-June 1934, p.
   6. They also varied greatly from month to month. See Earl
   Browder, *The Communist*, October 1934, p. 965. Another
   estimate of the relationship between dues payments and membership may be obtained from a report of Max Steinberg on
   New York District membership in July 1936, which reported
   12,870 dues payments while 15,814 members were carried on
   the rolls, a difference of about 20 per cent. *The Communist*,
   July 1936, p. 643. There has been talk of underground members not carried on party rolls, but there could not have been
   more than a handful of them.

   Access to dues-payments figures is rare. In any case, a better
   figure for membership is probably the number of registered
   members—all those registered at the beginning of the year, or
   on some other important occasion (*e.g.*, the reconstitution of
   the party in 1945).

   Rather higher figures than those in the table are sometimes
   found; for example, 74,000 for 1938, in the pamphlet by
   "Americus" (Earl Browder) called *Where Do We Go from*

Here?, November 6, 1948, p. 50. The source of this specific figure for 1938 is to be found in Jack Stachel's membership report to a meeting of the Central Committee in *The Communist*, March 1938, p. 220. He added to the 37,000 members registered in January 1937 the 37,000 recruited in almost fourteen months after that date. But from what is known of the high degree of "fluctuation," or turnover, in party membership, it would be reasonable to expect very heavy losses in new and old members by the time a new registration was completed. In the same report, indeed, Stachel said that only 55,000 of these 74,000 members had registered as yet in 1938.

Sometimes there is direct inflation of figures, but I have not found evidence of this in the party organizational reports. The exaggerations are in literature designed for a larger public than the regular party workers. For example, Earl Browder testified before the Special Committee on Un-American Activities in 1939 (U.S. House of Representatives, *Investigation of Un-American Activities in the United States, Hearings, Vol. 7*, 76th Congress, 1st Session, September 5, 1939, pp. 4283-4284) that "total membership . . . at present time" is 100,000. But he added, "I must qualify that by saying that of the present 100,000 . . . the amount of dues payments that reach the national office is . . . about 72 percent." However, testifying five years later before the Special Committee on Investigation of Campaign Expenditures (U.S. House of Representatives, *Investigation of Campaign Expenditures, Hearings, Part 4*, 78th Congress, 2nd Session, September 19, 1944, p. 66), Browder asserted that five years previously—at the time of the 1939 testimony—the party membership was 50,000. Perhaps Browder in 1939 also threw in the Young Communist League to get close to a round 100,000. Obviously, the figures could be built up by including more or less of the 20,000 or 30,000 who failed to maintain membership each year. In the same 1944 testimony, Browder said that membership two years before (1942) had been 55,000. *Ibid.*, p. 227. This was only 5,000 above the figure given in an internal unpublished membership report of 1942. But Browder also said that the membership at the time he was testifying was 80,000. *Ibid.*, p. 226. I prefer to use a calculation I have made from a report to the National Committee by Organization Secretary John Williamson. Even in cases of exaggeration, the differences are not large. I have one membership report—that for 1942—in the exact form in which it was given to high party officials. In that report it is asserted the party has a membership of 50,000, of which 44,000 have registered, and that this is the highest party membership in history. This brings into question Jack Stachel's specific assertion that 55,000 had already registered in early 1938, as well as Browder's statement in 1939. This is the only period (1938-39) for which there is evidence of some inflation of membership figures. If this membership report is compared with its published version (John Williamson in *The Communist,* May 1942, pp. 324-335), no distortion is found, though some figures, such as those of party membership just given, are omitted. It is interesting, too, that John Lautner's estimates, on the basis of knowledge available to high party officials, agree with those of the F.B.I. Lautner's estimates are somewhat higher, but the differences are not great.

For a general picture of the ebb and flow in party membership, and its rough dimensions at certain times, the figures in this table are, I believe, satisfactory.

The specific sources for the figures are as follows:

March-April 1930 through February 1933, and 1934: *Die Kommunistische Internationale vor dem VII. Weltkongress* (Moskau: Verlagsgenossenschaft ausländischer Arbeiter in der UdSSR, 1935), pp. 453-454; also, *Party Organizer,* May-June 1934, p. 6. *Party Organizer* gives specific figures; the report to the Communist International gives a range in which the *Party Organizer* figure is the upper limit.

July 1933 and May 1935: Jack Stachel, "Organizational Problems of the Party" (Abridged Report to the Meeting of the Central Committee, C.P.U.S.A., May 25-27, 1935), *The Communist,* July 1935, pp. 625-626.

October 1936: F. Brown, "Building the Party During the Election Campaign," *The Communist,* October 1936, pp. 968-969.

January 1937 and January 1938: Jack Stachel, "Build the Party for Peace, Democracy, and Socialism" (Report . . . at . . . Plenary Session of the Central Committee, C.P.U.S.A. . . . February 18-21, 1938), *The Communist,* March 1938, pp. 220-221.

April 1942: "Organization and Statistics, National Committee, April 5, 1942" (original document—Browder files).

January 1945: John Williamson, "New Organizational Problems of the Communist Party" (Report to the Meeting of the National Committee of the Communist Party, U.S.A., on November 17, 1945), *Political Affairs,* December 1945, p. 1122. (The calculation is on the basis of the statement, "If we can limit our losses to 10 percent [in re-registering the membership], we should have 58,000 members. If they reach 20 percent . . . only 51,000 members.")

January 1946: Henry Winston, "Toward a Party of 100,000," *Political Affairs,* January 1947, p. 67. (Calculated from the statement that the 20,000 recruited in 1946 represented "an increase of 38 percent.")

End of 1948 and January 1950: *Brownell* v. *Communist Party of the United States,* Subversive Activities Control Board Hearings, 1952, p. 9648.

1949 and 1950: F.B.I. estimates, quoted in Morris L. Ernst and David Loth, *Report on the American Communist* (New York: Holt, 1952), p. 33.

1951 and 1955: F.B.I. estimates, as given to Subcommittee to Investigate the Administration of the Internal Security Act . . . of the Committee on the Judiciary, United States Senate, *The Communist Party of the United States of America,* Document No. 117, 84th Congress, 2nd Session, 1956, pp. 34-35.

4. "The Seventh World Congress of the Communist International," *International Press Correspondence,* August 28, 1935, p. 1061.

5. John S. Gambs, *The Decline of the I.W.W.* (New York: Columbia University Press, 1932), pp. 82-91. The quotation is from p. 89.

6. See, for example, Joseph Freeman, *An American Testament* (New York: Farrar and Rinehart, 1936), Bk. III; and Whittaker Chambers, *Witness* (New York: Random House, 1952), pp. 191-259.

7. J. Peters, "Organizational Problems in the Light of the Open Letter," *The Communist,* September 1933, p. 953.

8. The argument for the importance of working-class opinion, in a period when the only apparent aim of the party was to influence public opinion, could become tortured: "A statement issued by a shop steward on the question of U.S.-Soviet collaboration for peace, on the seating of China in the United Nations,

on the withdrawal of American troops from Korea, backed by the support of workers in a department, is of more fundamental importance than a statement issued by this or that middle-class person who has no organized base in general and certainly no base among shop workers. . . . Does this mean that we counterpose what a shop steward does to what a writer does? It does not. In fact, both are necessary. I am simply saying that the action of workers in basic industry is decisive and that there is need for extending and enlarging upon working-class action which will in turn make possible more statements, more actions by writers, by professors and other groupings. . . ." Henry Winston, "Gearing the Party for Its Great Tasks," *Political Affairs*, February 1951, p. 31.

9. Speaking of a New York Section organizer known as "Julie," whose last name he was asked, William Cummings said: "I found out that at times he was known as Julie O'Connell and at times as Julie Katz." *Brownell* v. *Communist Party of the United States*, p. 9121. It was, of course, common, indeed almost universal, for party members to take party names. These tended to be of a blank general American character, concealing any specific ethnic background. Thus, it would be difficult to find Croatian background in the name of Steve Nelson, Finnish in that of Gus Hall, Jewish in that of Sam Darcy. This permitted the party cadre a wider range of roles from which to pick and choose.

10. The processes for doing this involved exhortation, propaganda, direct assignment, example, the experience involved in being thrown into work among elements one was not familiar with. But the importance of direct schooling should not be underestimated. During the early thirties, the Communists vigorously expanded a sizable school system for training cadres, as well as giving political orientation to the membership in general. This school system is described by Frank S. Meyer in *The Moulding of Communists* (New York: Harcourt, Brace, 1961), Chap. 9. The number that actually went to these schools was considerable. In May 1935, for example, Jack Stachel reported that 155 members had attended national training schools, 561 district training schools, 1,800 section training schools. These were all intensive, and the national, and perhaps the district, training schools involved full-time attendance for some length

of time. *The Communist,* July 1935, p. 627. Max Steinberg, reporting on the school work for New York, at a somewhat later period, said that 284 members in the New York District had attended full-time training schools, lasting for eight to ten weeks; 717 had attended part-time training schools; 1,328 had attended section training schools. *The Communist,* September 1938, p. 840. This was all aside from the public Workers School classes that were open to members and nonmembers and did not involve any intensive training.

11. John Roman, "Language Work in the Youngstown Section," *Party Organizer,* April 1934, p. 16.

12. *The Communist,* October 1931, p. 827. There is the same complaint in *Party Organizer,* July 1935, p. 10.

13. *Party Organizer,* May 1935, p. 11.

14. N. Stanton, "The Extraordinary Conference of the C.P. of the U.S.A.," *Communist International,* October 1933, p. 656.

15. All figures from *The Communist:* July 1935, p. 627; October 1936, p. 966; July 1936, p. 643; May 1935, p. 449; September 1938, p. 829.

16. *Ibid.,* May 1930, p. 419; June 1930, pp. 500-501.

17. *Ibid.,* June 1930, p. 528.

18. *Ibid.,* February 1932, p. 112.

19. *Ibid.,* September 1933, p. 950.

20. *Die Kommunistische Internationale vor dem VII. Weltkongress,* pp. 453-454.

21. *The Communist,* July 1935, p. 627.

22. *Ibid.,* October 1936, p. 968.

23. See *Die Kommunistische Internationale vor dem VII. Weltkongress,* pp. 453-454; *Party Organizer,* May-June 1934, p. 6.

24. Earl Browder, "The Struggle for the United Front" (Report to Meeting of the Central Committee of the Communist Party, September 5-6, 1934), *The Communist,* October 1934, p. 965.

25. *Die Kommunistische Internationale vor dem VII. Weltkongress,* p. 454.

26. *The Communist,* October 1934, p. 1005.

27. See John Williamson, "Some Burning Problems of Organization," *ibid.,* June 1930, p. 528; Max Steinberg, "Problems of Party Growth in the New York District," *ibid.,* July 1936, pp. 654-656.

28. There is another point on the problem of fluctuation which should be made. The turnover produced an ever-increasing

number of former Communists, many of whom made good potential material for future membership drives. Someone who had not registered one year might be got to re-register a year or two later. Thus, of 1,916 new members recruited in California in early 1937, 100 were former party members. *Ibid.*, April 1937, p. 19. It is known that some people who left the party on the occasion of one change of line might be induced to re-enter at another. Of course, many former Communists became violent opponents of Communism. And yet the greater part of the pool of former Communists served as a good fishing ground for new members, just as other radical groups (if they were not ideologically and strongly anti-Communist) might serve for the same purposes.

29. Note that such a vigorous activist as the young John Gates, arriving from New York, where he had been a student, in Youngstown in the early 1930's, could immediately throw himself into "unemployed work." John Gates, *The Story of an American Communist* (New York: Nelson, 1958), Chap. 3. It would have been infinitely harder for him to get into a factory. The unemployed were "open" to anyone who wished to take a leadership role among them. Since they had no "natural" social organization based on their circumstances, they also had no "natural" leaders. The situation was ready-made for outsiders— which is why the Communists were so successful.

30. John Williamson, "The Lessons of the Toledo Strike," *The Communist,* July 1934, pp. 644-646.

31. *Party Organizer,* January 1935, pp. 23-24.

32. *Ibid.,* July 1932, p. 7. See, too, an article on colonization in *ibid.,* April 1933, pp. 15-20.

33. Earl Browder, "Why an Open Letter to the Party Membership," *The Communist,* August 1933, pp. 759-760.

34. There are even complaints that the bosses know more about the workers than the Communist organizers do: ". . . during the strike wave that spread in the textile centers a few weeks ago . . . there was a very definite strike sentiment in Lawrence. The mill owners sensed it perhaps better than we did. They are in the mills with the workers day in and day out and often know the moods of the workers better than we do." *Party Organizer,* August-September 1933, p. 52.

35. For the labor policies of the twenties, see Draper, *The Roots of*

American Communism, pp. 198-200 *et passim;* and *American Communism and Soviet Russia,* pp. 215-233, 275-278, 285-296, 394-397. Howe and Coser, *op. cit.,* is also full on this subject; see pp. 73-82, 236-266.

36. See McAlister Coleman, *Men and Coal* (New York: Farrar and Rinehart, 1943), pp. 94-146; also James Wechsler, *Labor Baron: A Portrait of John L. Lewis* (New York: Morrow, 1944), pp. 27-28, 122-151.

37. Robert A. Christie, *Empire in Wood* (Ithaca, New York: Cornell University Press, 1956), pp. 260 ff.

38. This story is well documented. See Melech Epstein, *Jewish Labor in U.S.A.,* Vol. II, *1914-1952* (New York: Trade Union Sponsoring Committee, 1953), Chap. 8 and elsewhere; Joel Seidman, *The Needle Trades* (New York: Farrar and Rinehart, 1942), Chap. 9; Philip Foner, *The Fur and Leather Workers Union* (Newark: Nordan, 1950), pp. 110-684 (this book, a Communist account, is valuable if read with care).

39. Browder, *op. cit.,* 1933, p. 760.

40. J. Tsirol, "How the American Communist Party Carries Out Self-Criticism and Controls Fulfillment of Decisions," *Communist International* (British ed.), August 15, 1932, p. 515.

41. William Weinstone, "The XI Plenum of the Executive Committee of the Comintern," *The Communist,* October 1931, p. 795.

42. See Walter Galenson, *The CIO Challenge to the AFL* (Cambridge, Massachusetts: Harvard University Press, 1960), p. ix.

43. *Ibid.,* pp. 151, 478-486.

44. Sidney Lens, in *Left, Right and Center* (Chicago: Regnery, 1949), has a good description of this process, pp. 280-300. He points out that "Each time the membership of the various unions [organized in the first post–New Deal upsurge of labor organization in 1933 and 1934] dropped . . . the radicals of all shades and varieties hung on and consolidated their strength by taking over key posts." While the ordinary worker would join or leave a union in response to economic conditions, to the chances of the union to improve his state, and so on—in effect, for rational economic reasons—the radicals would join for reasons of ideological commitment. What few there were, were generally to be found in the unions, and consequently their

weight in the union was obviously greater than their weight in the industry.

45. Sam Darcy, "The Great West Coast Maritime Strike," *The Communist,* July 1934, p. 663.

46. *Ibid.,* pp. 679-680.

47. *Ibid.,* p. 682.

48. *The Communist,* October 1934, p. 965.

49. *Ibid.,* April 1937, p. 356.

50. *Party Organizer,* August-September 1933, p. 27.

51. David J. Saposs, *Communism in American Unions* (New York: McGraw-Hill, 1959), pp. 82-115; Matthew Josephson, *Union House, Union Bar* (New York: Random House, 1956), pp. 173 ff., 312 ff.

52. *The Communist,* March 1938, p. 225. Irving Howe and B. J. Widick, in *The UAW and Walter Reuther* (New York: Random House, 1949, p. 150), assert that "the actual C.P. 'fraction' [was never] more than 500."

53. See Galenson, *op. cit.,* Chap. 3; Howe and Widick, *op. cit.,* pp. 52-53, 70-80, 149-171; George Douglas Blackwood, "The United Automobile Workers of America, 1935-1951" (unpublished doctoral dissertation, University of Chicago, 1951); John Swift, "Reuther's Seizure of the Ford Local," *Political Affairs,* July 1952, pp. 7-23.

54. William Z. Foster, *History of the Communist Party of the United States of America* (New York: International, 1952), pp. 346-350. Foster claims that 60 of 200 full-time Steel Workers Organizing Committee organizers were Communists (p. 349). He describes a great conference of the organizations of the foreign-born, organized by Gebert in Pittsburgh, which brought together, in October 1936, 447 delegates representing 459,000 members. The claims may be exaggerated, but the Communists had influence among immigrant workers in Western Pennsylvania. This admission of the Communist role in the building of the C.I.O. was a late development, and itself part of the desperate attempt in the early fifties to retain some place for the Communists in the labor movement. At that time, the party regretted its concealment of its role. John Williamson wrote in 1951: "To this day the story has never been told of the role of our party in organizing the unorganized into the C.I.O. And, because we followed a wrong tactic of covering up the Communist identity of hundreds of C.I.O. organizers . . .

workers never knew our party's role. . . ." (*Political Affairs,*
February 1951, p. 71). See, too, William Goldsmith, "The
Communists and the International Workers Order," in *Studies
in Infiltration,* John P. Roche, ed. (forthcoming), p. 45; Bill
Gebert, "The Steel Drive and the Tasks of the Mass Organizations," *Party Organizer,* September 1936, pp. 12-15; Galenson,
op. cit., pp. 111 ff.

55. Galenson, *op. cit.,* pp. 111-112.
56. See Max M. Kampelman, *The Communist Party vs. the C.I.O.*
(New York: Praeger, 1957). For a detailed account of the
importance of tactical knowledge on the part of a union administration in fighting Communists (here the administration
was without such knowledge), see Vernon H. Jensen, *Nonferrous Metal Industry Unionism, 1932-1945* (Ithaca, New York:
New York State School of Industrial and Labor Relations,
1954). For an account of the alternative situation—where an
opposition, knowledgeable about Communist tactics, and with
the support of the national C.I.O., finally removed a Communist
administration—see Vernon H. Jensen, *Lumber and Labor*
(New York: Farrar and Rinehart, 1945), Chaps. 12 and 13;
and Galenson, *op. cit.,* pp. 389-408.
57. *The Communist,* January 1932, p. 114 (the districts for which
the occupations of those registered were given are: New York,
Cleveland, Detroit, Chicago, Minneapolis, Dakota, and Colo-
rado); *ibid.,* July 1935, pp. 625-626; March 1938, pp. 223-224;
"Organization and Statistics, National Committee, April 5,
1942."
58. On Communist recruitment of union activists, see Clayton
Fountain, *Union Guy* (New York: Viking, 1949), pp. 61 ff.;
Galenson, *op. cit.,* pp. 395-396; and Lens, *op. cit.,* pp. 229-231,
257-258.
59. George Morris, "Successful Recruiting Campaign of the
C.P.U.S.A.," *International Press Correspondence,* February 19,
1938, p. 139. See, too, Tim Ryan, "The National Recruiting
Campaign of the C.P.U.S.A.," *International Press Correspondence,* December 24, 1937, p. 1391, which says that *"hundreds*
[of these new members] are *trade union officials* of the lower
organizations" (italics in original).
60. These figures are calculated from those given in New York
District reports in *The Communist:* May 1935, p. 448; July
1936, p. 643; September 1938, p. 830. The New York District

membership consisted overwhelmingly of New York City members: in the 1938 New York State Convention, for example, only 9 per cent of the delegates came from places other than New York City. *Proceedings, 10th Convention, Communist Party, New York State* (New York: New York State Committee, Communist Party, 1938). The F.B.I. estimates may be found in Subcommittee to Investigate the Administration of the Internal Security Act, *The Communist Party of the United States of America*, p. 34.

61. "Organization and Statistics, National Committee, April 5, 1942."
62. *Political Affairs*, March 1946, pp. 233-234.
63. *Ibid.*, January 1945, pp. 49, 54.
64. *Ibid.*, December 1945, p. 1119. In *ibid.*, September 1946, p. 816, it was reported that this had been done.
65. *Ibid.*, September 1948, p. 842.
66. Committee on Un-American Activities, U.S. House of Representatives, *Colonization of America's Basic Industries by the Communist Party of the U.S.A.*, September 3, 1954, pp. 15-17, and *Investigation of Communist Activities in the State of Michigan, Parts 8, 9, 10*, 83rd Congress, 2nd Session, 1954.
67. It is interesting to note, too, that New York, despite its high proportion of white-collar and professional members, consistently had a higher proportion of party members who were trade-union members. This would reflect not their greater opportunity to join unions, but, rather, their more consistent carrying out of party policy, which demanded that each member join a union. In 1935, 55 per cent of the New York members were trade-union members, as against 35 per cent in Chicago, 27 per cent in Cleveland, 26 per cent in Detroit, 25 per cent in Pittsburgh. In 1942, 55 to 57 per cent of the New York members were in trade unions. The next highest proportion of trade-union members was in Pittsburgh (50 per cent); then came Philadelphia, 47 per cent; Ohio, 45 per cent; Illinois, 43 per cent, and other districts with lower trade-union memberships. *The Communist*, July 1935, p. 635; and "Organization and Statistics, National Committee, April 5, 1942."
68. The party was aware of this problem, but there seemed to be no way of building up the Communist elements in the Transport Workers Union. "In transportation we have a difficult task.

Ninety percent of the workers are Irish. However, in 1934 we had four members and now we have a unit in every shop in transportation. The biggest problem in transportation is red-baiting. There is the Catholic Church which sends its priests into the precincts to help in the red-baiting and at the present time they are forming every type of organization—the Holy Name, the Knights of Columbus, etc." *Party Organizer,* April 1938, p. 18. Max Steinberg, organizer for New York, complained: "The growth of the party in traction generally has in no way measured up to the tremendous achievements of the union." *The Communist,* September 1938, p. 833.

69. In two years, 1936-38, 600 seamen had been recruited in New York. As an indication of the quality of these members, the New York Maritime Section alone contributed 250 men to fight in Spain during the civil war. (The total number sent by the Communist Party to Spain has been generally given as 3,000.) See *Proceedings, 10th Convention, Communist Party, New York State,* pp. 21, 164. ". . . there were . . . about 500 party members among the 70,000-80,000 union members. Party members . . . controlled approximately 107 out of the 150 elected officials. . . ." David Dubinsky, as quoted in Kampelman, *op. cit.,* p. 84. On the nature of the struggle in the union, Curran asserted "that the Communists had spent $20,000 in the 1946 N.M.U. election, part of which was used to place their members 'on the waterfront on a full-time basis. . . .' " *Ibid.*

70. See the excellent discussion of these oddities in Galenson, *op. cit.,* Chap. 13.

71. S. M. Lipset, Martin Trow, James Coleman, *Union Democracy* (Glencoe, Illinois: Free Press, 1956), pp. 393-400.

72. S. M. Lipset, *Political Man* (New York: Doubleday, 1960), pp. 112, 194, 231, 234, 375.

73. Jensen, *Lumber and Labor,* pp. 269-270; Galenson, *op. cit.,* p. 406; Jensen, *Nonferrous Metals Industry Unionism,* pp. 108-121, 137.

74. See, for example, "The Party Position on Shop Papers" (*loc. cit.*), p. 3, which asserts that shop papers are now unnecessary. An editorial in the *Daily Worker* for March 27, 1939, says, "The Communist Party decided some time ago to abolish all fractions in the unions. . . ."

75. *The Communist,* October 1939, pp. 935-936.

76. *Ibid.,* September 1942, pp. 696-697.
77. John Williamson, in *ibid.,* July 1943, pp. 624-627; Earl Browder wrote forcefully to the same effect in *ibid.,* pp. 594-595.
78. Max Bedacht argued strongly in an interview with William Goldsmith and the author on May 3, 1957, that the abolition of the fractions led to the withering of the Communist rank-and-file in the trade unions, and the strengthening of the power of the Communist trade-union officials. The party leaders were then dependent on the union leaders, and could not control or undercut them by an appeal to the Communist rank-and-file, now left without organization. John Williamson makes a similar point in *Political Affairs,* January 1945, p. 52.
79. Herbert E. Krugman, "The Interplay of Political and Psychological Factors in Political Deviance" (unpublished doctoral dissertation, Columbia University, 1952), pp. 32, 54, 59.
80. *Political Affairs,* February 1951, pp. 51-52.
81. *Ibid.,* October 1953, p. 16.
82. The number of jobs controlled by the party was remarkable. Melech Epstein, in *op. cit.,* p. 234, wrote: "Early in 1939, this writer, discussing the matter with a few intimate friends in the party, reached the conclusion that not less than ten thousand people, in the unions, fraternal organizations, community centers, and in city, state and federal governments, owed their jobs, directly and indirectly, to the good will of the party." John Williamson gave a picture of the number of full-time Communist workers lost by the drafting of 12,000 members into the armed forces in *Political Affairs,* April 1945, p. 359. Those in the armed forces include "eighty-six full-time state officers, many times that number of County full-time officers, and the hundreds of full-time Communist trade union and other mass organization leaders." In the New York State Convention of 1938, of 766 delegates, 106 were full-time party functionaries, 253 were functionaries in mass organizations, 208 were functionaries in trade unions. *Proceedings, 10th Convention, Communist Party, New York State,* p. 301.

CHAPTER FOUR · JEWS AND MIDDLE-CLASS GROUPS AND THE
PARTY

1. An informed guess as to what part of the Communist Party during the later thirties and forties was Jewish could be made.
Melech Epstein makes one such over-all guess in a letter to
Werner Cohn used in the latter's doctoral thesis, "Sources of
American Jewish Liberalism" (The New School for Social Re-
search, 1956, pp. 134-136). But more important, perhaps, than
such a figure is an indication of the kind of material that permits a conclusion that the Jewish membership was large. For
example:

In *The Communist* for April 1929, Jack Stachel complained
that in Los Angeles "practically 90 per cent of the membership is
Jewish" ("Organization Report to the Sixth Convention,"
p. 183).

The New York State Convention delegates of 1938 were
analyzed by "national composition." Of the 766 delegates, it
was reported that there were: "Irish, 21; Italian, 44; Spanish,
Puerto Rican, Cuban, 6; West Indian, 7; German, 15; Chinese,
2; Philippine, 1." Elsewhere, it was reported that 11 per cent of
of the delegates were Negro. Thus, about 77 per cent of the
delegates are not accounted for by either race or national composition. It is also known that there was a tendency to over-
represent Negroes and underrepresented national groups at conventions. See *Proceedings, 10th Convention, Communist Party,
New York State* (New York: New York State Committee,
Communist Party, 1938), p. 301.

In 1945, John Williamson commented on the inadequacy
of the composition of the Brooklyn membership—this was
8,000, about one seventh, probably, of the party. He asserted
that the main base of the party in Brooklyn was in Brownsville,
Williamsburg, Coney Island, and Bensonhurst. "These are primarily Jewish American communities. . . . However, there
are certain areas that are almost exclusively proletarian and
non-Jewish in composition, as for instance, Greenpoint, Red
Hook, Bay Ridge, Sheepshead Bay, and Ridgewood. . . . In
these five areas our Party has only 201 members." *Political
Affairs,* March 1945, p. 236.

In 1948, there were approximately 10,000 party members in New York County. Jim Tormey, "Some New Approaches to Party Organization and Concentration Work," *The Communist,* June 1948, p. 552. Angela Calomiris, in *Red Masquerade* (Philadelphia: Lippincott, 1950), p. 203 gives 10,120. There were then 300 Italian party members in the county—a number which was considered much too small (*ibid.,* p. 200). Tormey complains about the few Negro members, but gives no figure (*op. cit.,* p. 552). Calomiris reports that only 100 Negroes were recruited in the previous year, 1947 (*op. cit.,* p. 202). From the relationship between Negro recruitment, losses, and membership (discussed in the next chapter), it would be a reasonable guess that at this time there could not have been more than about 300 Negro members. Further support for this estimate is found in the fact that in 1938, when the figure of Negro membership in New York was published (Max Steinberg, "Rooting the Party Among the Masses in New York," *The Communist,* September 1938, p. 829), it was 6 per cent of the district membership; in 1942, when it was not published, it was about 3 per cent ("Organization and Statistics, National Committee, April 5, 1942," Browder Files). If in 1948 it was not large enough to be proud of (that is, to be given), it was probably closer to 3 per cent than 6 per cent. Italians and Negroes were the most important ethnic and racial elements in New York County, after the Jewish. The Tormey report indicates general dissatisfaction with work among Puerto Ricans, Irish, Yugloslav-Americans (*op. cit.,* p. 555), as well as Italians. It would seem reasonable that a great majority of the party in New York County (one fifth of the entire party) was Jewish.

Aside from this material, which permits a statistical approximation of Jewish membership for certain areas, there are general complaints on this problem, too many to reprint. But here is a late complaint voiced at the 1951 convention of the Communist youth affiliate (Labor Youth League) in New York State: "The overwhelming strength [of our organization] does not now rest in the basic working class areas. We have a stronger LYL in Kings Highway than in Williamsburg [these are areas of Brooklyn; by 1951 a good part of the Jewish population was out of Williamsburg, where it had been so strong in 1945]. The Roll Call figures are higher in the West Bronx than in Prospect.

We have not made a decisive break among the Puerto Rican youth. We are isolated in the main from the Irish-American and Italian-American youth of New York." *Proceedings, First Empire State Convention, Labor Youth League* (New York: Labor Youth League, 1951), p. 7.

Sometimes there is a breakdown of a special group of leaders. For example: "Who are the educational workers? A study made of 34 educational workers (25 assembly district directors and nine county workers) who replied to a questionnaire, showed the following: . . . Russian—two; Jewish—17; Italian—two; American—nine." *Party Organizer*, February 1938, p. 34. (The "nationality" figures add up to only 30.)

Suggesting a much smaller proportion of Jewish members than any of the material quoted thus far is a report on national groups in the Browder files dated May 1938. This gives a general picture of the work being carried out in each group, and the membership in each group. For the Jewish group, it reports 4,000 members. While this is considerably larger than other large groups (German, 700; Italian, 600; Hungarian, 700; Ukrainian, 600; Lithuanian, 600-700; Finnish, 600; Greek, 600), these figures undoubtedly do not refer to all members of the given national origin, but only to the members engaged in the work of the specific national bureau. Presumably each bureau had its own approach to estimating membership—300 for the Croatian seems small.

2. The party may have known how many of the members were Jews, for it commonly took the ethnic background of a member into account in assigning the member to party work. For example, Angela Calomiris (*op. cit.,* p. 216) reports that she was not given a certain job because she was not a Yugoslav, while Matthew Cvetic was assigned to such work because he was (Committee on Un-American Activities, U.S. House of Representatives, *Exposé of the Communist Party of Western Pennsylvania, Hearings, Part I,* 81st Congress, 2nd Session, 1950, p. 1200). I have seen a membership registration form which requests "nationality" (in the archives of Kalman Marmor, in the Yiddish Scientific Institute in New York).

3. On the importance of the public face of the party, see Max Steinberg, "Problems of Party Growth in New York," *The Communist,* July 1936, p. 662: "We have pursued a conscious

policy of Americanizing the leadership of our Party. As contrasted with the last District Convention, today 45 per cent of our Section Organizers are native-born, as compared with the 100 per cent foreign-born in 1934." (There were thirty-one sections in the New York District when Steinberg made this report; there had been fourteen in 1934. *Ibid.,* p. 643.)

4. Attorney General Tom Clark in 1950 reported on a study of "4,984 of the more militant members of the Communist Party . . . as of 1947," and gave their national backgrounds. Subcommittee on Immigration and Naturalization, Committee on the Judiciary, U.S. Senate, *Communist Activities Among Aliens and National Groups, Hearings, Part I,* 81st Congress, 1st Session, 1950, pp. 318-320. Forty-four per cent were of Russian stock (born in Russia, or having at least one Russian parent) or were married to persons of Russian stock. An additional 12.5 per cent were of stock of countries adjacent to Russia, or married to persons of such stock. Seventy-eight and a half per cent were of foreign white stock, 37 per cent of Russian stock, 11.5 per cent of stock of countries adjacent to Russia, 30 per cent of other foreign white stock. Most of those of Russian stock and of stock of the countries adjacent to Russia were Jewish. But the Department of Justice did not give this figure.

5. Lipset, Trow, and Coleman have gone as far as any sociologists have in differentiating the significance of religion in forming a social milieu from other factors affecting political outlook. Even they, in a work which must stand as a model of the lengths to which the analysis of a sample can be carried, would find it difficult to separate, *within* the Jewish milieu, the significance of religio-cultural elements and social elements, the product of a special history. S. M. Lipset, Martin Trow, James Coleman, *Union Democracy* (Glencoe, Illinois: Free Press, 1956), pp. 326-329 and elsewhere.

6. On the socio-economic rise, see Nathan Glazer, "Social Characteristics of American Jews," *American Jewish Year Book,* Vol. 56 (New York: American Jewish Committee, 1955), pp. 3-41, and works there cited; and S. M. Lipset and Reinhard Bendix, *Social Mobility in Industrial Society* (Berkeley, California: University of California Press, 1959), p. 306 (subject index on "Jews"). On liberalism, see Cohn, *op. cit.,* and works cited therein; and Lawrence H. Fuchs, *The Political Behavior of American Jews* (Glencoe, Illinois: The Free Press, 1956).

7. See Melech Epstein in Cohn, *op. cit.*, p. 134, for the Russian Federation.

8. In one of the rare government remarks about the number of Jews in the Communist Party, a House investigating committee asserted in 1931, "A large percentage of all known district organizers are of Jewish origin." (At this time there were about twenty district organizers, and the district organizers are the most important level of leadership below the top national leadership.) See Special Committee to Investigate Communist Activities in the United States, U.S. House of Representatives, *Investigation of Communist Propaganda,* Report No. 2290, 71st Congress, 3rd Session, January 17, 1931, p. 14.

9. This is a difficult impression to substantiate, but there is no evidence of any important Jewish aspect to the unemployed work, which was the main source of party recruitment in the early thirties; and in the absence of such evidence, which is to be found in so many other areas of the party's work, it may be assumed that it represents some real absence of impact on Jews. It is interesting that of the ten biographies of leaders in unemployed work in Chicago given in Harold Lasswell and Dorothy Blumenstock, *World Revolutionary Propaganda* (New York: Knopf, 1939), pp. 283-292, not a single one is Jewish. This is surprising enough, in the light of the general distribution of Jews and non-Jews throughout the party, to suggest either that Jews were consciously excluded from this selection of biographies or that, as I believe, Jews did not figure prominently in this work. It was also in this period that New York supplied a relatively small proportion of the membership.

10. Robert W. Iversen, *The Communists and the Schools* (New York: Harcourt, Brace, 1959), Chap. II.

11. "In the early thirties there were about 850,000 teachers in the country. Of these, only about 5,000 were organized into the American Federation of Teachers, and about a fourth of these were in Local 5, the New York Teachers Union. . . . There were over 30,000 teachers in New York. . . ." *Ibid.,* p. 32. In 1935, the A.F.T. had 9,683 members, the New York local 2,131 members. *Ibid.,* p. 53. In 1936, the union had 15,000 members, the New York local 3,000. *Ibid.,* p. 103.

12. Jews were prominent in all the radical factions in the union. Note that all the "Rank-and-File" (Communist) leaders up on trial before the union in 1932 (*ibid.,* p. 38) appear to be Jewish,

as were the five members of the editorial staff of the *New York Teacher* removed by the Communists after their victory because they belonged to the Lovestoneite opposition (*ibid.*, p. 112). It is somewhat dangerous to argue ethnic identification on the basis of names, but these seem to be unambiguous.

13. *Ibid.*, pp. 37 (Communists and Lovestoneites), 53-54 (Communists and Socialists).

14. *Ibid.*, pp. 127-128. But not all Socialists and Lovestoneites cooperated with Communists. It was generally a strictly limited cooperation for specific ends, and, after 1934, became less common and soon disappeared.

15. See Glazer, *op. cit.*, pp. 20-23.

16. S. M. Lipset and Juan Linz, in *The Social Bases of Political Diversity in Western Democracies* (Stanford, Calif., Center for Advanced Studies in the Behavioral Sciences, 1956, mimeographed), argue (Chap. XI, p. 38) that social workers are the most Left of all professions. They cite (Chap. XI, p. 20) a report—Alice I. Bryan, *The Public Librarian: A Report of the Public Library* (New York: Columbia University Press, 1952), mimeographed version—that 17 per cent of librarians in the spring of 1948 preferred Socialist, Communist or Progressive Party candidates for President—suggesting a rather Leftist group.

17. Iversen, *op. cit.*, Chap. III.

18. Jacob Fisher, *The Rank and File Movement in Social Work, 1931-36* (New York: New York School of Social Work, 1936), pp. 7-8.

19. On the whole development of union activity among groups of professional and white-collar workers, see the articles by Vera Shlakman, in *Science and Society:* "White Collar Unions and Professional Organization," XIV (1950), pp. 214-236; "Unionism and Professional Organization among Engineers," XIV (1950), pp. 322-337; "Business and the Salaried Worker," XV (1951), pp. 97-121; "Status and Ideology of Office Workers," XVI (1952), pp. 1-26. These articles do not speak of the Communist role in these developments.

20. Fisher, *op. cit.*, p. 9. See, too, the role of Jewish social workers in developing unionization, pp. 16 and 35.

21. *Proceedings of the Second Convention of the United Office and Professional Workers of America* (New York: U.O.P.W.A.,

1938), p. 18; *Proceedings of the Third Convention, United Office and Professional Workers of America, C.I.O.* (New York: U.O.P.W.A., 1940), pp. 30-31.

22. See the valuable report by Lucy Dawidowicz, *The Social Service Employees Union: Communist Infiltration through a Trade Union Movement* (New York: American Jewish Committee, March 6, 1951, mimeographed).

23. *Proceedings of the Second Convention of the U.O.P.W.A.*, p. 18.

24. This was in the course of a discussion of Jewish work among Communists, not trade-union activity. The reporter takes it for granted that the extension of the Teachers Union means the extension of Communist influence.

25. *Proceedings, 10th Convention, Communist Party, New York State*, p. 205. These general figures of party membership were confirmed some years later by the proceedings of the Board of Education of New York City under the state law requiring the dismissal of teachers who were members of the Communist Party. Between 1953 and 1958, 447 teachers were involved in these proceedings: 33 were dismissed, 249 resigned when summoned for questioning, 34 resigned while their cases were under consideration, 126 convinced the Board of Education they had left the party, and 5 were testing one of the decisions of the Board in the courts. During the same period, 122 teachers under the Board of Higher Education had been investigated, with varying results. Iversen, *op. cit.*, p. 340. Independently of proceedings under the state law, thirty-seven teachers had been fired or resigned earlier because of actions arising from the activities of the Rapp-Coudert Committee. See Iversen, *op. cit.*, pp. 215-216. Some other teachers were also fired for taking the Fifth Amendment before Congressional committees. The total was more than 600 teachers in New York City who were at one time or another members of the Communist Party. If one adds persons who left the teaching profession before these investigations (by 1953, inflation had made teaching jobs much less attractive), then Bella Dodd's figure of "close to 1,000 Party members in a union of 4,000 members" in early 1941 does not seem unreasonable. *School of Darkness* (New York: Kenedy, 1954), p. 130. It can be seen what a high concentration of party members existed in the Teachers Union. In Congressional testimony, Miss Dodd repeated this figure of 1,000,

and said there were 1,500 Communist Party teachers in the entire country. Iversen, *op. cit.,* p. 317.

Were the 600 teachers uncovered by official investigations members of the party at the same time? The quotation in the text indicates there were only thirty-five Communists in the union in 1935. This suggests that whatever teachers were to enter the party did so rapidly in the next few years, and while there were, of course, losses and gains, it seems reasonable to assume that most of the teachers charged under the investigations were in the party during the same period, in the late thirties and forties.

John Lautner also testified as to the existence of a large group of teachers in the party at the end of the forties. He was responsible for the reorganization of the party into groups of three for security purposes. Of possibly 500 members in the New York City school system, he asserted, 300 had been re-grouped in the new structure of threes by the time of his expulsion in 1950. *Brownell* v. *Communist Party of the United States,* Subversive Activities Control Board Hearings, 1952, pp. 9353, 9358.

The number of teachers in the Communist Party may also be calculated from sources independent of those given to date— from official membership reports of the party. There are a number of occasions when teachers were listed as a separate group in these reports, instead of being placed in such categories as intellectuals, professionals, and the like. In May 1935, Jack Stachel reported to the Central Committee on "Organizational Problems of the Party" (*The Communist,* July 1935, pp. 625-640). A registration covering 27,000 members revealed 425 teachers. In a report to the Central Committee delivered in February 1938 (in *ibid.,* March 1938, pp. 220-241), Stachel analyzed 17,000 new recruits who had come into the party since the preceding June. In this group, there were no less than 440 teachers. It is clear that the proportion of new teachers among recruits of late 1937 was greater than the proportion of teachers in the party in 1935 (2.6 per cent against 1.6 per cent). The number of teachers recruited in 1937 added to teachers in the party in 1935 makes 865 teachers. Of course there must have been drop-outs from the earlier group, as well as recruitment (and further drop-outs) in 1935, 1936, and

1937. But it is interesting that a variety of estimates of teachers in the party in the late thirties are within the same order of magnitude—from 600 (investigations in the 1950's) or "many hundreds" (1938 New York State Convention) to 1,000 (Bella Dodd).

26. Personal interview, June 23-24, 1957.

27. Glazer, *op. cit.,* p. 24.

28. See Melvin J. Fagen, "The Status of Jewish Lawyers in New York City," *Jewish Social Studies,* 1 (1939), pp. 73-104.

29. Personal interview with Frank Meyer and Elsie Meyer, Summer 1957.

30. Committee on Un-American Activities, U.S. House of Representatives, *Communist Activities Among Professional Groups in the Los Angeles Area, Hearings, Part I,* 82nd Congress, 2nd Session, 1952, pp. 2571-2572. This testimony asserts that these thirty lawyers formed one fifth of the membership of the National Lawyers Guild in Los Angeles. In 1951, the National Lawyers Guild had 2,100 members, about 40 per cent in New York. *Ibid.,* p. 2661. If the same proportion of Communists to the membership as a whole prevailed as in Los Angeles, this would mean 420 Communist lawyers.

31. Herbert A. Philbrick, *I Led 3 Lives* (New York: McGraw-Hill, 1952), pp. 238, 240.

32. See Irving Howe and Lewis Coser, *The American Communist Party, a Critical History: 1919-1957* (Boston: Beacon, 1957), Chap. VIII.

33. Israel Amter, "New Organizational Forms Prove Their Value," *The Communist,* May 1936, pp. 537-541. On the organizational change, see the decision on organization, *Party Organizer,* January 1936, pp. 8-10; F. Brown, "Improved Organization Forms Will Make Recruiting Drive More Effective," *ibid.,* December 1935; Max Steinberg, "Organize to Strengthen and Build the Party," *ibid.,* January 1936; I. Amter, "Organizational Changes in the New York District of the Party," *The Communist,* May 1936, pp. 465-473; F. Brown, "New Forms of Party Organization Help Us Win the Masses," *Party Organizer,* July-August 1936, pp. 7-11.

34. *Party Organizer,* December 1935, p. 15.

35. *The Communist,* November 1935, p. 1010.

36. Not that the response necessarily followed the party theory.

Herbert E. Krugman finds that his trade-union Communists tended to join in "Right" periods, the "intellectuals" in "Left" periods ("The Interplay of Political and Psychological Factors in Political Deviance," unpublished doctoral dissertation, Columbia University, 1952, p. 58).

37. "Win the Masses in *Their* Organizations," *Party Organizer*, December 1935, p. 18.

38. *The Communist*, March 1935, p. 251; *Party Organizer*, September 1937, p. 6.

39. *Party Organizer*, July 1937, p. 6. There were then 3,400 members in the Detroit District, giving an average membership per unit of fifteen.

40. *The Communist*, September 1938, p. 328.

41. *Ibid.*, April 1939, p. 328.

42. *Political Affairs*, November 1944, p. 1024. See, too, John Williamson's "The Role of the Club in the Communist Political Association," *ibid.*, July 1944, pp. 608-613.

43. John Williamson, "The Reconstitution of the Communist Party," *ibid.*, September 1945, pp. 806-808.

44. Melech Epstein, *The Jew and Communism* (New York: Trade Union Sponsoring Committee, 1959), Chap. 28.

45. Nathan Glazer, *American Judaism* (Chicago: University of Chicago Press, 1957), Chap. VI.

46. "On the Communist Approach to Zionism, a Reply to a Memorandum," *The Communist*, July 1936, pp. 666-670. The line is kept firm in articles by Paul Novick in *ibid.*, June 1936, September 1938, and May 1940 (after the Nazi-Soviet pact), and an article by M. Welnar in *ibid.*, August 1939.

47. Melech Epstein, *op. cit.*, pp. 365-366.

48. *The Communist*, August 1940, p. 709.

49. International Workers Order Files on the J.P.F.O., dealing with the American Jewish Congress and the American Jewish Conference; William Goldsmith, "The Communists and the International Workers Order," in *Studies in Infiltration*, John P. Roche, ed. (forthcoming).

50. *Political Affairs*, October 1945, p. 928.

51. Alexander Bittelman, *Program for Survival: The Communist Position on the Jewish Question* (New York: New Century, 1947), pp. 16, 52-53. The resolution appears in this pamphlet, as also in *Political Affairs*, October and November 1946.

52. See, for example, in the I.W.O. files the exchange between David Petegorsky of the Congress and Rubin Saltzman of the J.P.F.O., April 23, 1947, and April 29, 1947.

53. *Political Affairs,* February 1948, pp. 146-155; August 1948, pp. 720-730.

54. David A. Shannon, *The Decline of American Communism* (New York: Harcourt, Brace, 1959), pp. 157-158; Samuel Lubell, *The Future of American Politics* (New York: Double-day-Anchor, 1956), pp. 91-93.

55. Shannon, *op. cit.,* pp. 180-181; Lubell, *op. cit.,* pp. 219-220.

56. *Political Affairs,* March 1949, pp. 72-86.

57. Goldsmith, *op. cit.,* p. 85.

58. Solomon M. Schwarz, "The New Anti-Semitism of the Soviet Union," *Commentary,* June 1949, pp. 535-545.

59. John Williamson, *Political Affairs,* July 1950, pp. 58, 63.

60. F. Brown, "For Improving the Work of the Party Among the Foreign-Born Workers," *The Communist,* July 1934, pp. 700-710, is the last general article on this part of the party's work to appear in *The Communist* until the development of the new party line on national groups three years later.

61. Earl Browder, "The Communists in the People's Front," *ibid.,* July 1937, pp. 623, 625.

62. Earl Browder, *Report to the Eighth Convention, Communist Party* (New York: Workers Library, 1934), pp. 96-97; and *Report to the Ninth Convention of the Communist Party* (New York: Workers Library, 1936).

63. "It is clear that if we Communists adopt this individualized, specialized approach to the various groups, *finding points of agreement rather than disagreement,* we will be able to make big inroads. . . ." "Significance of the Coming Municipal Elections," I. Amter, *The Communist,* July 1937, p. 658. Not that the Communists were above appeals to national feeling earlier. *Party Organizer,* July 1935, pp. 21-23, reports effective use in a German neighborhood in New York of the Saar question. But this was rare.

64. Earl Browder, *The Democratic Front: Report to the Tenth National Convention of the Communist Party of the U.S.A.* (New York: Workers Library, 1938), pp. 53-60, 73-74.

65. *Resolutions of the Tenth Convention of the Communist Party, U.S.A.* (New York: Workers Library, 1938), p. 20.

66. "Work Among National Groups—A Central Communist Task," by I. Amter, *The Communist,* August 1938, pp. 722-731.

67. Irene Browder, "For a Correct Approach to the Problems of National Groups" (Report delivered May 27, 1938, at the Commission on National Groups, Tenth Convention, C.P.-U.S.A.), *The Communist,* September 1938, pp. 797-804; "Problems of the National Groups in the United States," *ibid.,* May 1939, pp. 456-466; "The National Groups in the Fight for Democracy," *ibid.,* September 1939, pp. 857-866.

68. "Resolutions of the National Committee, in Plenary Session, February 17-18, 1940," *ibid.,* March 1940, pp. 230-231; "The Reactionary Political Role of the Vatican," by Louis F. Budenz, *ibid.,* May 1940, pp. 431-450 ("We can increase our cooperation with Catholic masses by stressing the question of a united, independent Ireland," p. 449); Louis Budenz, *This Is My Story* (New York: McGraw-Hill, 1947), pp. 204-208; testimony of Louis Budenz and John Huber, in Subcommittee on Immigration and Naturalization, Committee on the Judiciary, *Communist Activities Among Aliens and National Groups, Hearings, Parts I and II,* pp. 237 ff., 522-525.

69. Israel Amter, "The National Groups: A Powerful Force in the Struggle Against Fascism," *The Communist,* August 1940, pp. 712-723; A. Landy, "The National Groups in the National Front," *ibid.,* October 1941, pp. 917-936.

70. Between 1928-29 and 1934-35, these schools grew only slowly —from thirty-two schools and 2,213 pupils in the first period to fifty schools and 2,644 pupils in the second period. *1936 Jewish Education Survey* (New York: Committee for Jewish Education, 1936, mimeographed), p. 74. In 1948, at their peak, there were more than 100 schools, and 7,000 students. Goldsmith, *op. cit.,* p. 82.

71. Philip Foner, "The Jew in America's Struggle for Democracy," in *Our People: The Jew in America* (New York: Co-Operative Book League, Jewish-American Section, I.W.O., 1944), pp. 9-103.

72. *Ibid.,* p. 210.

73. On the American Slav Congress, and these wartime currents among Slavic groups, see Committee on Un-American Activities, U.S. House of Representatives, *Report on the American Slav Congress and Associated Organizations,* House Report No.

1951, 81st Congress, 2nd Session, June 26, 1949; Subcommittee on Immigration and Naturalization, Committee on the Judiciary, *Communist Activities Among Aliens and National Groups,* throughout; A. Landy, "A Year of American Slav Unity," *The Communist,* June 1943, pp. 552-566; Goldsmith, *op. cit.,* Chaps. IV and V.

74. "Some of the staunchest Communists [in the South Slav work] are . . . American-born, and they speak English better than they do Serbian or Croatian." Subcommittee on Immigration and Naturalization, Committee on the Judiciary, *Communist Activities Among Aliens and National Groups, Hearings, Part II,* p. 616; see, too, *Part I,* p. 378, for reference to important native-born Slovak leaders. Cvetic, though born in the United States, was at this time directed to work in the Slovene group and the American Slav Congress. Committee on Un-American Activities, *Exposé of the Communist Party of Western Pennsylvania, Hearings, Part I,* p. 1700.

75. Israel Amter, in *The Communist,* August 1941, p. 722: The State Committees "must immediately release capable, politically developed forces, especially the American-born among the national groups, for this work." John Williamson, *Political Affairs,* April 1945, p. 365: "In the field of the national groups there is a real dearth as far as new and growing Communist cadres are concerned. Each District [should] take bold steps to assign young native-born comrades . . . to give leadership to the work."

76. Cvetic testimony, Committee on Un-American Activities, *Exposé of the Communist Party of Western Pennsylvania, Hearings, Part I,* p. 1206.

77. Article by Israel Amter, *Daily Worker,* July 4, 1948; Gus Hall, "For a Marxist-Leninist Leadership in the National Groups Field," *Political Affairs,* September 1950, pp. 30-36; Henry Winston, "Gearing the Party to its Tasks," *ibid.,* February 1951, p. 32.

78. George Jure Prpic, "The Croats in America" (unpublished doctoral dissertation, Georgetown University, 1959), pp. 329-331. Communist influence had been strong in this organization for a long time; a report on national group work in the Browder files dated March 1938 asserts that more than 40 per cent of the lodges of this order were under party influence.

79. It is difficult to document the general observation that Jews broke disproportionately from the party after 1956. I have

made some calculations of the proportion of Jews among important members who left the party in Southern California, on the basis of a Committee on Un-American Activities report (*Report on the Southern California District of the Communist Party,* U.S. House of Representatives, 86th Congress, 1st Session, April 3, 1959). Of a group of fourteen leading members who resigned from the party in March 1958, at least nine were Jewish (pp. 24-27). A list of other leading party personalities (pp. 32-35), probably representative of party activists in general, containing seventy-six names, is about half Jewish. This suggests that the Jews were disproportionately represented among party activists leaving at this time, as they were among better-known party leaders and intellectuals.

80. Note, too, that the editors of the *Daily Worker,* mostly Jewish, were more outraged by the revelation of the destruction of Jewish culture in the Soviet Union than the editors of *Jewish Life,* the magazine conducted by the Jewish specialists of the party. Shannon, *The Decline of American Communism,* pp. 284-285.

81. The literature on this subject is enormous. To refer only to books that deal wholly or in large part with the relationship between the intellectual and cultural worlds and Communism: Eugene Lyons, *The Red Decade* (New York: Bobbs-Merrill, 1941); Joseph Freeman, *An American Testament* (New York: Farrar and Rinehart, 1936); Whittaker Chambers, *Witness* (New York: Random House, 1952); Granville Hicks, *Where We Came Out* (New York: Viking, 1954); Howard Fast, *The Naked God* (New York: Praeger, 1957). See, too, Howe and Coser, *op. cit.,* Chap. VII. There are thousands of pages of testimony taken from writers, professors, theater and movie people, composers, and others by the various Congressional committees. Here it is only necessary to establish the general fact of this pervasive influence.

82. The literature on this question is also large. See Raymond Aron, *The Opium of the Intellectuals* (London: Secker and Warburg, 1957); Jules Monnerot, *The Sociology and Psychology of Communism* (Boston: Beacon, 1953); and Richard Crossman, ed., *The God That Failed* (New York: Harper, 1949). There are many articles: note Michael Polanyi, "The Magic of Marxism," *Encounter,* 39 (December 1956), pp. 5-17.

83. Cohn, *op. cit.,* pp. 11-13.

CHAPTER FIVE · NEGROES AND THE PARTY

1. On the subject of the Negroes in the Communist Party there are two full-length books: Wilson Record, *The Negro and the Communist Party* (Chapel Hill, North Carolina: University of North Carolina Press, 1951), and William A. Nolan, *Communism Versus the Negro* (Chicago: Regnery, 1951). Theodore Draper, in his *American Communism and Soviet Russia* (New York: Viking, 1960), devotes a long chapter (15) to a complete and definitive account of the formation of the American Communist line on the Negroes in the 1920's. Record has written a second book-length manuscript (unpublished), "The Communist Party and the National Association for the Advancement of Colored People." In view of this extensive secondary literature on the subject, this chapter is limited only to the discussion of American Negro membership in the party, and some of the problems related to it.

2. Draper, *op. cit.*, p. 321.

3. *Ibid.*, p. 349.

4. John Albert Morsell, "The Political Behavior of Negroes in New York City" (unpublished doctoral dissertation, Columbia University, 1950), pp. 37 ff.

5. Draper, *op. cit.*, pp. 331, 471, n 44.

6. There are two excellent accounts of social relations between Negroes and whites in the Communist Party: Richard Wright's essay in *The God That Failed,* edited by Richard Crossman (New York: Harper, 1949); and Claude McKay, *Harlem* (New York: E. P. Dutton, 1940).

7. There is a good description of the Yokinen trial in Irving Howe and Lewis Coser, *The American Communist Party, a Critical History: 1919-1957* (Boston: Beacon, 1957), pp. 209-211. The Browder quotation is from *The Communist,* March 1933, p. 242. Yokinen, it appears, was really not such a ferocious white chauvinist: pointing out that the Yokinen trial had educated the membership, Harry Haywood wrote: "Comrade Yokinen himself . . . after six months, came back into the Party as one of the staunchest fighters for the program of Negro liberation and . . . as a result of his courageous and militant stand on this question was deported by the Negro-hating imperialist

government." *Ibid.*, September 1933, p. 893. The play acting of this early uproar over white chauvinism is in sharp contrast with what happened after 1949, when the expulsions for white chauvinism were much more seriously meant, and helped deplete the party. See David A. Shannon, *The Decline of American Communism* (New York: Harcourt, Brace, 1959), pp. 242-247.

8. B. Sherman, "The Eighth Convention of the Communist Party of the U.S.A. and Some Conclusions," *Communist International,* June 1934, p. 390. The party then had about 10 per cent of its membership Negroes, according to Sherman (p. 393), but 17 per cent of the delegates were Negro. The party was supposed to make up a delegation to a Profintern (Communist trade-union conference) in 1930 that was one third Negro, but did not have enough to get this proportion. Fred Beal, *Proletarian Journey* (New York: Hillman-Curl, 1937), pp. 245-249.

9. A. Markoff, "Role of Party Training Schools in Developing Leadership," *The Communist,* July 1931, p. 629; "The Training of New Cadres and Our School System," *ibid.,* August 1932, p. 732.

10. Harold Lasswell and Dorothy Blumenstock, *World Revolutionary Propaganda* (New York: Knopf, 1939), p. 239.

11. Wright, *op. cit.* (Bantam Books edition), p. 128.

12. For a brief account of the Communist use of the Scottsboro case, see Howe and Coser, *op. cit.,* pp. 212-216. For the Communist management of a later case, see William Goldsmith, "The Communists and the International Workers Order," in *Studies in Infiltration,* John P. Roche, ed. (forthcoming). On the use of the Scottsboro case to recruit party members, see *Party Organizer,* May-June 1933, pp. 14, 17.

13. William Z. Foster, *History of the Communist Party of the United States* (New York: International, 1952), p. 269; *The Communist,* April 1929, p. 184; August 1930, p. 688; June 1930, p. 500; October 1931, pp. 793, 803.

14. *The Communist,* February 1932, p. 114.

15. *The Communist,* July 1935, p. 627.

16. *Ibid.,* March 1938, p. 233; *Party Organizer,* June 1938, p. 2; "Organization and Statistics, National Committee, April 5, 1942" (Browder files). *The Communist,* June 1943, p. 540, June 1944, p. 521; *Political Affairs,* September 1946, p. 813.

17. Foster, *op. cit.*, p. 479. He is contradicted by other party sources. For example: "Alex Parker," *Organizing the Party for Victory over Reaction* (New York: New Century, 1953), p. 31, who says, "Since the end of the war, we have had a continuous decline in Negro membership." And in 1949, an F.B.I. agent asserted there were then only 1,400 Negroes in the party. Committee on Un-American Activities, U.S. House of Representatives, *Hearings Regarding Communist Infiltration of Minority Groups—Part I,* 81st Congress, 1st Session, 1949, p. 426.

18. *The Communist,* July 1936, pp. 645-646. The proportion of Negroes in the New York District rose from 4.5 per cent in 1934 to 6.5 per cent in 1936 and to 7 per cent in 1938. *Ibid.,* July 1936, p. 643; September 1938, pp. 829-830. The Negro percentage among recruits ran at about twice this figure. *Ibid.,* December 1937, p. 1137. By 1942, the percentage in New York was down to 3. Meanwhile, Chicago continued to remain the strongest district in Negro membership outside the South; in 1942, it had a Negro percentage of twenty-one. "Organization and Statistics, National Committee, April 5, 1942."

19. "Alex Parker," *op. cit.,* p. 47.

20. *Political Affairs,* April 1945, p. 365.

21. *Political Affairs,* July 1945, pp. 621-622.

22. *Brownell* v. *Communist Party of the United States,* Subversive Activities Control Board Hearings, 1952, pp. 9377-9378.

23. Committee on Un-American Activities, U.S. House of Representatives, *The American Negro in the Communist Party,* December 22, 1954, p. 1.

24. George Blake, "New York's 1949 Elections," *Political Affairs,* December 1949. Despite the 1949 losses, the article reports (p. 52): "The bulk of the American Labor Party vote still comes from the Jewish voters. . . . The drift toward the Liberal Party could have been checked by more effective work among the Jewish people. . . . The A.L.P. losses among the Jewish voters . . . had its roots in the long period of neglect by the Communist Party and the progressive movement of struggle on issues affecting the Jewish people. . . ." But a year later, the Negro emphasis was as strong as ever, and George Blake wrote: "The nomination of Dr. DuBois against Lehman created confusion among large sections of traditional supporters of the American Labor Party in the labor movement, among

the Jewish communities, and in the Negro communities as well."
Political Affairs, January 1951, pp. 30-31. On the impact of
the white-chauvinism campaign on Jewish Communists, see,
for example, Committee on Un-American Activities, *Hearings
Regarding Communist Infiltration of Minority Groups—Part I,*
p. 441.

25. Irving Howe and B. J. Widick, *The U.A.W. and Walter
Reuther* (New York: Random House, 1949), pp. 223-225. John
Williamson, "The Trade Unions and the Negro Workers,"
Political Affairs, November 1947, lists unions with and without
Negroes in top positions, and emphasizes the importance of
making this a general issue (p. 1012).

26. Henry Winston, "Party Tasks Among the Negro People,"
Political Affairs, April 1946, p. 354, discussed this policy, and
commended a local of the United Electrical, Radio & Machine
Workers of America for adopting a special provision on layoffs
for Negroes. John Williamson, in *ibid.,* June 1949, pp. 32-35,
discussed the Communist position on this issue. The importance
of this issue is again stressed in "The Struggle for Jobs and for
Negro Rights in the Trade Unions," by Hal Simon, in *ibid.,*
February 1950, p. 37 ff.

27. Note an unpublished doctoral dissertation by John Graves
("Reaction of Some Negroes to Communism," Teachers College, Columbia University, 1955), who interviewed 512 Negroes
on the streets of Harlem, between September 1952 and December 1954. At that time, the overwhelming majority of Americans
were hostile to Communism: he found 61 per cent sympathetic
(p. 88), and found that the more educated (who presumably
knew more about what went on in the Communist Party, what
kind of policies it had, what happened to Negro visitors in
Russia), were even more sympathetic (p. 96).

28. Draper, *op. cit.,* pp. 315-316.

29. James Q. Wilson, *Negro Politics* (Glencoe, Illinois: The Free
Press, 1960), pp. 3-5.

30. See Ralph Lord Roy, *Communism and the Churches* (New
York: Harcourt, Brace, 1960), pp. 202-203, 422.

31. On National Urban League, see testimony of Lester Granger,
Committee on Un-American Activities, *Hearings Regarding
Communist Infiltration of Minority Groups—Part I,* pp. 467 ff.
On the N.A.A.C.P., see Record, "The Communist Party and

238 Notes: pages 187-191

the National Association for the Advancement of Colored People."

1. "Reference group" is a sociological term that refers to the group or condition—past, present, or future, real or imaginary —with which a given group makes a comparison in evaluating its circumstances. Thus, generals may feel discontented if their reference group is generals in other countries, contented if their reference group is colonels in their own.
2. On this matter of how a single generation is given by its experiences a certain political outlook which it may retain through its entire lifetime, see Marvin Rintala, "The Problem of Generations in Finnish Communism," *American Slavic and East European Review,* 17, 1958, pp. 190-202.
3. Even so, this pre-existing Socialist world, buried by the twenties, could be called upon by the Communists in their work. It is interesting to run across references in the party literature of the thirties to the manner of work in the small towns and among the farmers: the organizer looks up, to begin with, the former Socialists. As to why "there is no socialism in the United States," I will not add to this widely discussed question. For the best statement I know on this problem, see Martin Diamond, "Socialism and the Decline of the American Socialist Party" (Ph.D. thesis in political science, University of Chicago, 1956). See, too, for an interesting analysis of the radical differences between Marxism and the fundamental characteristics of American thinking and patterns of social action, Clinton Rossiter, *Marxism: The View from America* (New York: Harcourt, Brace, 1960).
4. Philip Selznick, in *The Organizational Weapon* (New York: McGraw-Hill, 1952), and *Leadership in Administration* (Chicago: Row, Peterson, 1957), and various articles; S. M. Lipset, with Martin Trow and James Coleman, in *Union Democracy* (Glencoe, Illinois: The Free Press, 1956), and various articles.
5. Diamond, *op. cit.,* pp. 69-70.

INDEX